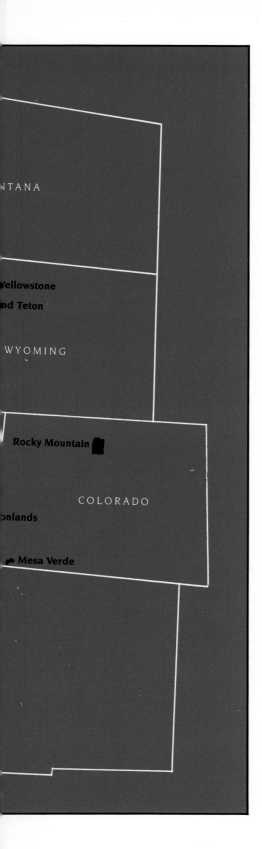

▲ △   Campgrounds

△   Cabins

■   Visitor Center

□   Ranger Station

〜 Road

⌒ Dirt or Unmaintained Road

⌐ ⌐ ⌐ ⌐ Trail

Visiting
Our Western
National Parks

BY
GEORGE P. PERKINS

To Gail

Whose tireless effort made the book a reality

Introduction

Visiting Our Western National Parks is designed to help the tourist plan his or her trip to our western parks. Basically, all the information about each park is readily available at the particular park itself. However, it has been my experience that there is very little information at any one park about the facilities of another. Also it is my belief that many people do not know to whom or where to write to obtain the information that they desire while planning their trip.

Our parks are administered in a very professional manner and many regulations are consistent throughout the system; however, by the same token, each park has its own individual personality which also translates into its special regulations.

Other countries are envious of what we have. Our national parks are unique to the world and internationally famous. As evidence, one hears many languages when visiting our parks. They are a natural treasure that should be protected from ourselves. There remain many challenges, particularly in those parks where wildlife is the main attraction. Huge concentrations of people and the natural ecology do not mix well, and the National Park Service has the unenviable responsibility of striking a balance.

I hope you enjoy visiting our national parks as much as I have.

GEORGE P. PERKINS

Foreword

The National Park Service was officially established on August 16, 1916. However, national parks had been in existence for nearly 45 years. Congress passed legislation establishing some 13 individual national parks and 24 monuments before establishing a national park "service". The Acts of Congress in no way preceded the public's natural curiosity, and many hardy souls in buckboards and stagecoaches penetrated the wildernesses of the Yellowstones and Yosemites to experience the wonderments of truly unique aboriginal environments.

For the most part, early park visitors were left to their own resources, since little or no money was available for the operation of the parks. Consequently, a tradition of professional guides developed with varying degrees of honesty and integrity. Some provided accurate and factual information about the natural and physical features of a particular area that the traveler was about to enter. But others relied on an endless collection of folk tales, legends and conjecture.

As the national parks matured and became more accessible, the spectrum of their visitors also expanded. The off-the-cuff remark by well-meaning "neighbors" no longer satisfied the informational needs of the expanded National Park Service public. The wealth of scientific data that became available also expanded and continues to do so.

The knowledge and sensitivity required to produce a visitor-oriented guide is not common in most writers. Relatively few are able to capture and retell an experience that is meaningful to the average visitor. George Perkins has been a long-time resident of the Lassen area, and his interest in backpacking and photography has given him a very personal insight into the ecological essence that the hiker becomes emersed in as he moves along a backcountry trail. In his previous book, *Hiking Trails of Lassen Volcanic National Park*, he recreates this experience in an understandable conversation that is both factual and yet entertaining. His efforts to produce this and other guides are not motivated by profit but by his personal desire to share with park visitors the near inspirational experiences that are possible in the national parks.

RICHARD L. VANCE
Chief Naturalist
Lassen Volcanic National Park

As the popularity of the parks and the sophistication of their visitors continued to increase through the years, it became necessary to employ park rangers whose main responsibility was to accumulate and disseminate scientific information pertaining to the geology, flora, ecology, etc. of the parks. The exhibits, campfire programs, conducted hikes, and other interpretive functions we all enjoy today are a result of the efforts of these dedicated personnel titled Park Naturalists or Park Interpreters.

I would like to thank the following National Park Service personnel for their help in editing the material for this book:

Anna Marie Fender	Arches National Park
Margaret Littlejohn	Bryce Canyon National Park
J. Jerry Rumburg	Canyonlands National Park
George Davidson	Capitol Reef National Park
William S. Gleason	Capitol Reef National Park
William H. Ehorn	Channel Islands National Park
Cindy Nelson	Channel Islands National Park
Kent Taylor	Crater Lake National Park
Clyde M. Lockwood	Glacier National Park
John C. O'Brien	Grand Canyon National Park
Patrick Smith	Grand Teton National Park
Albert J. Hendricks	Great Basin National Park
James Boll	Haleakala National Park
Tom White	Hawaii Volcanoes National Park
Jon Erickson	Hawaii Volcanoes National Park
Richard L. Vance	Lassen Volcanic National Park
Marilyn Coyler	Mesa Verde National Park
William F. Dengler	Mt. Rainier National Park
Ronald G. Warfield	Mt. Rainier National Park
Loren Lane	Mt. Rainier National Park
John R. Douglass	North Cascades National Park
Henry "Hank" Warren	Olympic National Park
Sharon I. Wray	Olympic National Park
Terry E. Maze	Petrified Forest National Park
Lori Heinsohn	Petrified Forest National Park
Richard A. Rasp	Redwood National Park
Glen Kaye	Rocky Mountain National Park
John J. Palmer	Sequoia/Kings Canyon National Parks
George B. Robinson	Yellowstone National Park
Leonard W. McKenzie	Yosemite National Park
Lisa T. Dapprich	Yosemite National Park
Marla LaCass	Yosemite National Park
Victor L. Jackson	Zion National Park

Table of Contents

Arches

LOCATION:	Southeastern Utah
ACCESS:	Hwy. 191, 5 miles northwest of Moab, UT
SEASON:	All year
HOURS:	24 hours/day
ENTRANCE FEES:	$5/vehicle/week (includes admission to Canyonlands); $2/person all others/week; $15 annual; $25 Golden Eagle
GAS, FOOD & LODGING:	Moab
NEAREST PROPANE:	Moab
CAMPGROUNDS:	Devil's Garden: 53 individual sites and 2 group sites; no hook-ups; $5 fee
ADJACENT FACILITIES:	Complete commercial facilities in Moab, UT; see below for RV parks
VISITOR CENTER:	Arches Visitor Center at Park Entrance
MUSEUM:	In Arches Visitor Center
PICNICKING:	Visitor Center; Devil's Garden; Balanced Rock

TOURS:	Fiery Furnace Walk daily spring and summer; self-guiding auto tour booklet available
ACTIVITIES:	Hiking; backpacking (free permit required); interpretative programs; horseback riding*; jeep tours*; educational seminars* *Concession operated
CLIMATE:	Hot summers; cold winters
ELEVATION:	4,000 to 5,700 ft.
SIZE:	115 sq. miles
ANNUAL VISITATION:	Approximately four hundred thousand
PETS:	Must be on leash; not permitted on trails
FACILITIES FOR DISABLED:	Visitor Center; restrooms
INFORMATION:	*Supt. Arches National Park* 125 W., 200 S. *Moab*, UT 84532 801/259-8161

CAMPGROUND

Devil's Garden (elev. 5200') is the only campground in the Park. It is located 18 miles N of the Visitor Center just off the main Park Road. It has 53 individual sites for both tents and trailers and 2 group campsites for 10 to 55 persons at a cost of $2/person (reservations required). Facilities include tables and firepits. The campground is open all year, with water and flush toilets from mid-March to mid-October and chemical toilets and no water in winter. The fee is $5 per night in summer and limit of stay is 14 days. The campground is on a first-come basis and usually fills by mid-afternoon during the summer months. There is an amphitheater with nightly interpretive programs in the summer, and the campground is useable for the handicapped. Gathering of firewood is forbidden.

ADJACENT FACILITIES

KOA:Moab: 4 mi. S on Hwy. 191; open all year; full hook-ups; showers; propane; store; laundry; ice; reservations: 3225 S Hwy. 191, Moab, UT 84531; 801/259-6682

Slickrock Country: 1 mi. N on Hwy. 191; open all year; full hook-ups; showers; propane; store; cafe; laundry; ice; reservations: P.O. Box 1236, Moab, UT 84532; 801/259-7660

Canyonland Campark: on Hwy. 191 in Moab; open all year; full hook-ups; showers; store; laundry; ice; reservations: 555 S. Main, Moab, UT 84532; 801/259-6848

Big Sky Campground: 5 mi. N on Hwy. 191; open all year; store; ice

HIKING

Most of the hiking trails consist of short hikes from the roads to the various arches. There are backpacking hikes available (permits required) and backpacking regulations are provided. Most of the hikes are easy—well-suited for families with children or the elderly.

Klondike Bluffs and Herdina Park are available to four-wheel-drive vehicles. Klondike Bluffs can also be reached through Salt Valley on 9 miles of unpaved road, which turns off main Park road .1 mi. S of the trailhead to Skyline Arch. Do not travel unpaved roads when wet or when thunderstorms are imminent.

From Main Park Road

Devil's Garden: (one way) to TUNNEL ARCH 0.25mi/0.4 km; to PINE TREE ARCH 0.25mi/0.4km; to LANDSCAPE ARCH 1mi/1.6km; to WALL ARCH 1.2mi/1.9km; to PARTICIAN ARCH 1.7mi/2.7km; to NAVAJO ARCH 1.7mi/2.7 km; to DOUBLE O ARCH 2.0mi/3.2km; trailhead:. North end of main Park road. If you are only going to take one hike, this should be it. The 2¼ mi. trail ends at Dark Angel, a large rock pinacle. Another trail returns for 2.1 mi. to Landscape Arch via Fin Canyon. (It's another mile back to the trailhead.) The route is marked by stone trail markers.

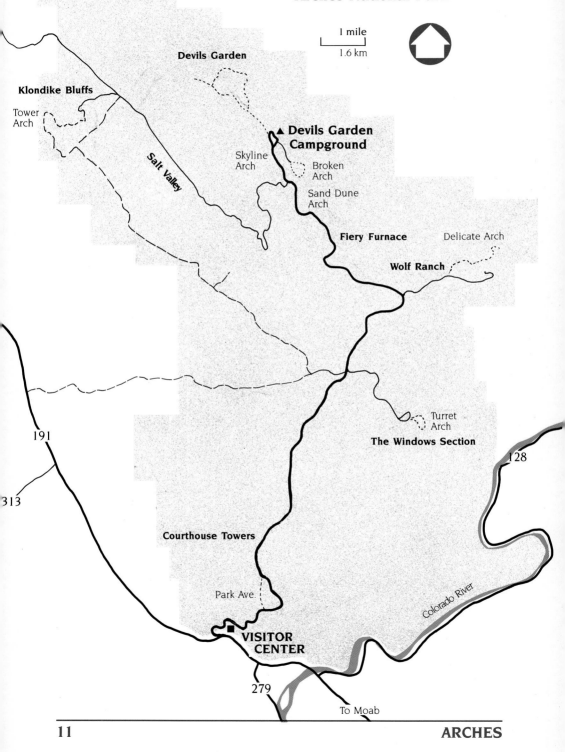

Arches National Park

1 mile
1.6 km

Devils Garden

Klondike Bluffs

Tower
Arch

Salt Valley

Skyline
Arch

▲ Devils Garden
Campground

Broken
Arch

Sand Dune
Arch

Fiery Furnace

Delicate Arch

Wolf Ranch

191

313

Turret
Arch

The Windows Section

128

Courthouse Towers

Park Ave.

Colorado River

■ VISITOR
CENTER

279

To Moab

ARCHES

Park Avenue Trail: 1.0mi/ 1.6km; 30 minutes; trailheads: South or North Park Avenue. This trail is usually hiked one way with a car pick-up at the other end.

Skyline Arch: .2mi/.3km; trailhead: One-half mile S of Devil's Garden trailhead.

Sandune Arch: .2mi/.3km; trailhead: Approximately 1½ mi. S of Devil's Garden trailhead.

Broken Arch: .5mi/.8km; trailhead: Approximately 1½ mi. S of Devil's Garden trailhead.

Balanced Rock: .3mi/.5km; trailhead: Across the road from the 4-wheel-drive exit to Klondike Bluffs.

From Windows Area

Turret Arch, South and North Window: .2mi/.3km

Double Arch: .3mi/.5km

From Wolf Ranch

Delicate Arch Trail: 100 yds. to Wolf Cabin; 1.5mi/2.6km to Delicate Arch, the Park's most famous and photographed Arch.

Delicate Arch View Point: 1.2mi/1.9km (of road). Note: You can hike up a moderately steep trail for a closer view of Delicate Arch.

From Klondike Bluffs

Tower Arch: 1.5mi/2.6km; trailhead: Klondike Bluffs parking area. The trail goes past Marching Men formation.

BRIEF HISTORY

The first humans to occupy the Arches area were the Fremont and Anasazi Indians. The area was marginal for both hunting and agriculture, however, and was abandoned by them around A.D.1300. An early white settler of Arches was John Wesley Wolfe who, in 1888, built a cabin on Salt Wash below Delicate Arch; the cabin still stands.

Alexander Ringhoffer is credited with being the father of Arches National Park. He guided railroad officials to Klondike Bluffs in 1923 with the idea of making it a tourist attraction. The idea caught on and through Stephen Mather, the first Director of the National Park Service, Arches was proclaimed a National Monument on April 12, 1929 by President Hoover. On November 16, 1971, the bill establishing Arches National Park was signed into law by President Nixon.

AUTHOR'S COMMENTS

The geology of the Park is mainly Entrada and Navajo Sandstone, and the erosional forces of wind, water, freezing and thawing have, through millions of years, formed the arches. There are over 500 identifiable arches in the Park. While the desert ecology may seem barren to the average visitor, it literally teems with plant and animal life which has adapted to the harsh conditions.

The beautiful salmon-colored arches and massive pinacles produce a feeling of reverence similar to being in a cathedral.

Bryce Canyon

LOCATION: South central Utah

ACCESS: From east, on Utah 12 to Utah 63; from west, on US 89 to Utah 12 and Utah 63

SEASON: All year; main roads open in winter

HOURS: 24 hours/day except for roads to Fairyland Point and Rainbow Point, which close at sundown

ENTRANCE FEES: $5/vehicle/14 days; $2/person all others/14 days; $15 annual; senior citizens and handicapped (US citizens) free; $25 Golden Eagle

GAS & FOOD: In park during summer months; surrounding area (within 7 miles) rest of year

LODGING: BRYCE CANYON LODGE: mid-May through September; rooms and cabins; dining; reservations: TW *Services, Inc.*, 451 N. *Main St., Cedar City,* UT 84720; 801/586-7686.

NEAREST PROPANE: Bryce Canyon Country Store and Campground

CAMPGROUNDS: Two campgrounds; some year-round sites; no hook-ups; showers and laundromat nearby

ADJACENT FACILITIES: See below

VISITOR CENTER: Bryce Canyon Visitor Center by Entrance Station (8—4:30 year round except Christmas Day; extended hours in summer)

MUSEUM: Exhibits in Visitor Center

PICNICKING: Near North Campground; Sunset Point; Park road south of East Creek; park road near Whiteman connecting trail; Rainbow Point

GIFT SHOP: In Bryce Canyon Lodge

TOURS: Ranger-guided walks and talks; van tours in summer; snowshoe tours in winter (available only by prior arrangement and appointment with the Chief Naturalist)

ACTIVITIES: Hiking; backpacking (permit required); horseback riding; snowshoeing and cross-country skiing; interpretive programs; scenic flights (offered outside the park only)

CLIMATE: Spring—fall warm days, cool nights; winter cold with snow.

ELEVATION: 6,600 to 9,100 ft.

SIZE: 56 sq. miles

ANNUAL VISITATION: Approximately three-quarters million

PETS: Must be on leash; not permitted in canyons or public buildings

FACILITIES FOR DISABLED: Most buildings and viewpoints; all restrooms; Rim Trail between Sunrise and Sunset Points

INFORMATION: *Supt. Bryce Canyon National Park*
Bryce Canyon, UT 84717
801/834-5322
Park Emergency: 801/676-2411 (collect)

*NOTE: Day visitors must park trailers in the Visitor Center parking lot, as no trailers are allowed beyond Sunset Campground.

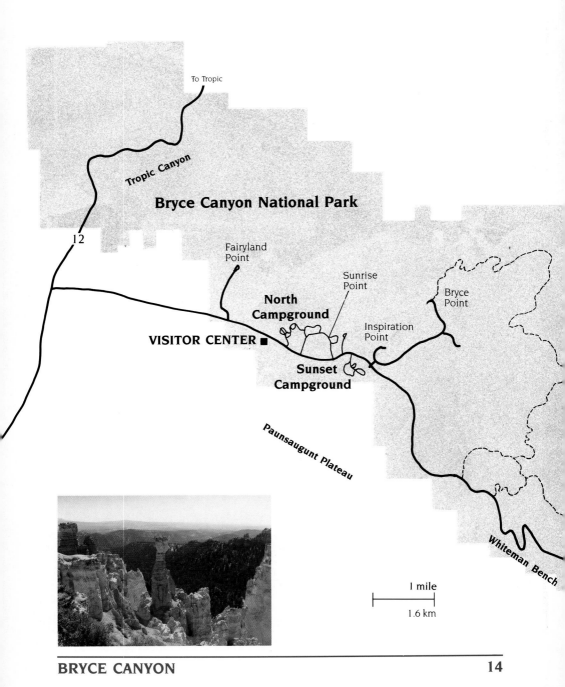

To Tropic

Tropic Canyon

Bryce Canyon National Park

12

Fairyland
Point

Sunrise
Point

Bryce
Point

**North
Campground**

VISITOR CENTER ■

Inspiration
Point

**Sunset
Campground**

Paunsaugunt Plateau

Whiteman Bench

1 mile

1.6 km

CAMPGROUNDS

- All campsites are on a first-come basis and have a 14-day limit of stay.
- The fee is $5 per night.
- There are tables and grills at each campsite and a nearby store, showers and laundromat.
- The campgrounds have modern comfort stations with water and flush toilets and amphitheaters with evening campfire programs during summer months.
- Wood gathering is prohibited; wood is for sale at the gas station during summer months.
- Parts of the campgrounds are handicapped accessible.

North (elev. 8000') is located approximately .2 mi. S of the Entrance Station in a wooded area. It has 111 sites and part is open all year. The campground usually fills by late afternoon during summer months. Facilities include a dump station.

Sunset (elev. 8000') is located 1 mi. S of North Campground in a forested area. It has 107 individual sites, 1 group site (reservations required) and is open June through Labor Day.

ADJACENT FACILITIES

Best Western Ruby's Inn: Approximately 1.5 mi. N of Park boundary; large resort with full line of services including RV park with hook-ups, and expanding; reservations: 801/834-5341

Red Canyon Forest Service Campground: In Dixie National Forest 3 miles past the turn-off from Hwy. 89 onto Hwy. 12; open 4/15 to 11/15; wooded campground with comfort stations, tables and grills.

Bryce Canyon Country Store and Campground: Approximately 10 mi. E of Hwy. 89 on Hwy. 12; full hook-ups; showers; gas; propane; ice; reservations: 801/834-5218

Riverside Cg & RV Park: 1 mi. N of Hatch on Hwy. 89; open 5/15 to 10/31; full hook-ups; showers; flush toilets; propane; dump station; cafe; ice; reservations: Box 576, Hatch, UT 84735; 801/735-4223

Red Canyon RV Park: On Hwy. 12 1 mi. E of junction with Hwy. 89; open 4/1 to 11/1; full hook-ups; showers; flush toilets; store; cafe; ice; reservations: Box 717, Panguitch, UT 84759; 801/676-2672

Pink Cliffs Village: Lodging; camping; restaurant; groceries; laundromat; showers; ice; reservations: 801/834-5303

Bryce Canyon Pines: Lodging; restaurant; 801/834-5336

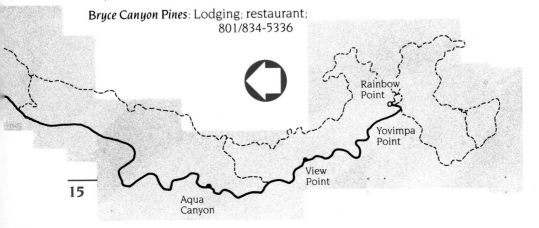

Rim Trail: 5.5mi/8.9 km one way; 2−2½ hours; easy to moderate; 550' descent; trailhead: anywhere between Fairyland Point and Bryce Point. This trail skirts the Bryce Canyon amphitheater with many fabulous views. Any section may be walked, and between Sunrise and Sunset Points the trail is suitable for wheelchairs.

Queen's Garden Trail: 1.5mi/2.4km round trip: 1−2 hours; moderate; 320' descent; trailhead: Sunrise Point. This trail offers views of Queen Victoria, Gulliver's Castle, etc.

Navajo Loop Trail: 2.2mi/3.5km round trip; 1−2 hours; moderately strenuous; descent 521'; trailhead: Sunset Point. The trail descends to Two Bridges and past Thor's Hammer Trail ending at Wall Street, where 1984 rock slide is visible.

Queen's Garden/Navajo Trail Combination: 3.0mi/4.8km one way; 2−3 hours; moderately strenuous; descent 521'; trailhead: Either Sunrise Point or Sunset Point (makes a loop). This is one of the best trails for viewing the canyon's scenery and the park's many wildflowers. It's advisable to start at Sunset point— water at the trailhead and an easier climb out to Sunrise Point.

Peekaboo Loop: 5−7mi/8−11.3km; 3−4 hours; strenuous pedestrian and horse trail; 500−800' descent; trailheads: Bryce, Sunset or Sunrise Points. The loop lies in the bottom of the canyon and features spectacular scenery, including Peekaboo Box Canyon and Wall of Windows.

Tower Bridge Trail: 3.0mi/4.8km; 2½ hours; strenuous; 800' descent; trailhead: just north of Sunrise Point. The trail descends among Bristlecone Pines past the Chinese Wall to Tower Bridge.

Fairyland Loop Trail: 8.0mi/12.9km; 5 hours; strenuous; 900' descent; trailheads: either Fairland View or just north of Sunrise Point. This little-hiked trail views the Chinese Wall, Tower Bridge, the remains of Oastlers Castle, and circles around the base of Boat Mesa.

Hat Shop Trail: 3.8mi/6.0km; 3−4 hours; strenuous; 900' descent; trailhead: Bryce Point. This little-used trail descends to an area of many pillars, each capped by a "hat".

Bristlecone Loop Trail: 1.0mi/1.6km; 1 hour; easy to moderate; 100' descent; trailhead: Rainbow Point. This trail offers spectacular views across southern Utah through Bristlecone Pine, White Fir and Spruce trees.

Riggs Spring Loop Trail: 8.8mi/14.2km round trip; 4−5 hours strenuous; 1675' descent; trailhead: Yovimpa Point. This trail descends to the valley below through a forest of aspen, white fir, maple, Gambel oak and huge ponderosa pine. Breaks in the trees offer excellent views of the colored cliffs above.

Under-the-Rim Trail: 22.6mi/36.2km one way; 2−3 days; strenuous; 1500' descent; trailhead: Bryce Point; end: Yovimpa Point (or vice versa—can be hiked either way). This is considered the main backpacking trail in the park. There are a number of connecting trails to the road, for those who desire a shorter hike. Free overnight camping permits are required. No fires are allowed.

GENERAL HIKING NOTES

Bryce is basically a day-hike park with many inter-connecting trails which may be utilized to extend hikes. Backpacking is mainly associated with the Under-the-Rim or Riggs Spring Loop Trails.

During the summer months, it is best to do your hiking early in the day and auto touring in the afternoon because of the cool mornings. Driving the Rainbow Point Park road for 15 miles south offers a number of viewpoints—Farview Point, Natural Bridge, Aqua Canyon and Ponderosa Point. In the Bryce Amphitheater, viewpoints accessible by auto are Fairyland, Sunrise, Sunset, Inspiration, Bryce, and Paria Points.

One suggestion is to view the sunrise from Sunrise Point and then, as the sun rises, hike the Queen's Garden Trail. The official sunrise time is available at the Visitor Center.

Always carry water and wear a hat. The 7,000−9,000 ft. elevation combined with warm summer temperatures can cause dehydration. And sturdy hiking shoes/boots are always recommended.

BRIEF HISTORY

The Anasazi Indians were probably the first Indians to visit the area which is now the park. They hunted and gathered here and departed some 1,000 years ago. Thereafter, the Paiutes followed and utilized the area for the same reasons.

Early Spanish explorers looking for a route between New Mexico and California probably viewed the pink cliffs in 1776. Early American pathfinders Jedediah Smith, George Yount, and John C. Fremont explored near the park area in the early to middle 1800's. The southern end of the Paunsaugunt Plateau was explored by John Wesley Powell in 1879. Bryce Canyon is named for Ebenezer and Mary Bryce, who homesteaded in the area around 1875.

Through the efforts of J.W. Humphrey and others, the public was made aware of the unique beauty of this area. Bryce Canyon National Monument was created June 8, 1923. It became Utah National Park on June 7, 1924 and became Bryce Canyon National Park on September 15, 1928.

AUTHOR'S COMMENTS

Bryce Canyon National Park, in the author's opinion, combines many features that enhance it as an outstanding park. Warm, pleasant days and cool nights provide an invigorating climate. The park can be easily viewed by foot, auto, wheelchair, stroller or helicopter.

Bryce Canyon is not a canyon but a plateau (Paunsaugunt) within a plateau (Colorado). The sediment from ancient Lake Flagstaff was uplifted some 16 million years ago and formed the Colorado Plateau. Then erosion, mainly in the form of snow, rain and ice, worked away the weaker, softer rock to form the strikingly beautiful and inspiring rock formations we see today. The top appears level, but as the mantle of beautiful huge ponderosa pine gives way to aspen and white fir on driving south to Rainbow Point, over 1,000 ft. elevation is surprisingly gained.

Canyonlands

LOCATION:	Southeastern Utah
ACCESS:	From Moab, U.S. 191 and Utah 313 to Island in the Sky Visitor Information Center (31 miles); from U.S. 191, take Utah 211 36 mi. west to The Needles; from Utah 24 or 95, take 2- and 4-wheel-drive routes east to The Maze
SEASON:	All year
HOURS:	24 hours/day
ENTRANCE FEES:	$5/vehicle/week (good for all districts of Canyonlands as well as Arches National Park); $2/person all others/week; $15 annual; $25 Golden Eagle
GAS, FOOD & LODGING:	Moab, Monticello, Green River, Hanksville
NEAREST PROPANE:	Moab, Monticello
CAMPGROUNDS:	Two developed campgrounds; numerous primitive campgrounds in remote areas (permit required)
ADJACENT FACILITIES:	See below
VISITOR CENTERS:	Park Headquarters, 125 W. 200 S., Moab, UT; Information Centers at Monticello and all 3 districts
PICNICKING:	Several designated sites with tables, grills, toilets but no water; also at option throughout park
TOURS:	Four-wheel-drive tours; river float trips; bus tours; sightseeing flights; interpretive campfire programs at Island in the Sky and Needles
ACTIVITIES:	Hiking; horseback riding; rafting (permit required to run Cataract Canyon); mountain biking; four-wheeling
CLIMATE:	Hot in summer (June/July/August highs 100+ degrees); cold in winter (Jan/Feb lows 0–10 degrees)
ELEVATION:	3,700 to 7,000 ft.
SIZE:	527 sq. miles
ANNUAL VISITATION:	Near two hundred thousand
PETS:	Must be on leash; not permitted on trails
FACILITIES FOR DISABLED:	Limited (some restrooms and pathways)
INFORMATION:	*Supt. Canyonlands National Park* *125 W. 200 South* *Moab, UT 84532* 801/259-7164

The entrance for this District is on Utah 313, which turns off US 191 approximately ten miles north of Moab, UT. The road is narrow and steep in places. The Visitor Information Station is a little over two miles inside the Park boundary.

CAMPGROUNDS

Willow Flat Campground (elev. 6128') is located 28 mi. from the junction of US 191 and Utah 313. It has 12 sites and is open all year. Facilities include tables, grills and pit toilets. There is no water at this campground. Camping is on a first-come basis with no fee, and limit of stay is 14 days. Wood-gathering is prohibited.

HIKING

TRAIL	TRAILHEAD	LENGTH ONE WAY	TIME ROUND TRIP
*Shafer Canyon Overlook	.5 mi. S of ranger station	.2mi/.3km	15-30 min.
* Neck Spring	.5 mi. S of ranger station	5.0mi/8.0km	3-5 hrs.
Lathrop	1.8 mi. S of ranger station	9.0mi/14.4km	4-7 hrs.
*Mesa Arch	6.0 mi. S of ranger station	.5 mi. loop	30 min.
Murphy	Murphy Road— 9 mi. S of ranger station	4.5mi/7.2km	6-8 hrs.
White Rim Overlook	11.3 mi. S of ranger station	.75mi/1.2km	1 hour
Government	11.3 mi. S of ranger station	2.5mi/4km	3-4 hrs.
Grandview	12.3 mi. S of ranger station	.75mi/1.2km	30-60 min.
Monument Basin	contact ranger	1.7mi/2.8km	3-4 hrs.
Aztec Butte	Upheavel Dome Road	.5mi/.8km	1 hour
Wilhite	Upheavel Dome Road	5mi/8km	3-6 hrs.
Alcove Spring	Upheavel Dome Road	5mi/8km	3-5 hrs.
Whale Rock	Upheavel Dome Road	.25mi/.4km	20-30 min.
Syncline Valley loop	Upheavel Dome Road	4.0mi/6.4km	3-4 hrs.
*Upheavel Dome Overlook	Upheavel Dome Road	.5mi/.8km	30-60 min.
Upheavel	Upheavel Dome Road	3.5mi/5.6km	2-4 hrs.

 * Self-guiding Trails

More detailed information on the hiking trails is available at the ranger station.

ADJACENT FACILITIES

In Moab, UT (see Arches National Park)

Dead Horse Point State Park: Adjacent to park on Utah 313; open all year; $3/vehicle fee; CAMPGROUND: open April-Oct.; 21 sites; $6/night camping fee; water; flush toilets; dump station

---

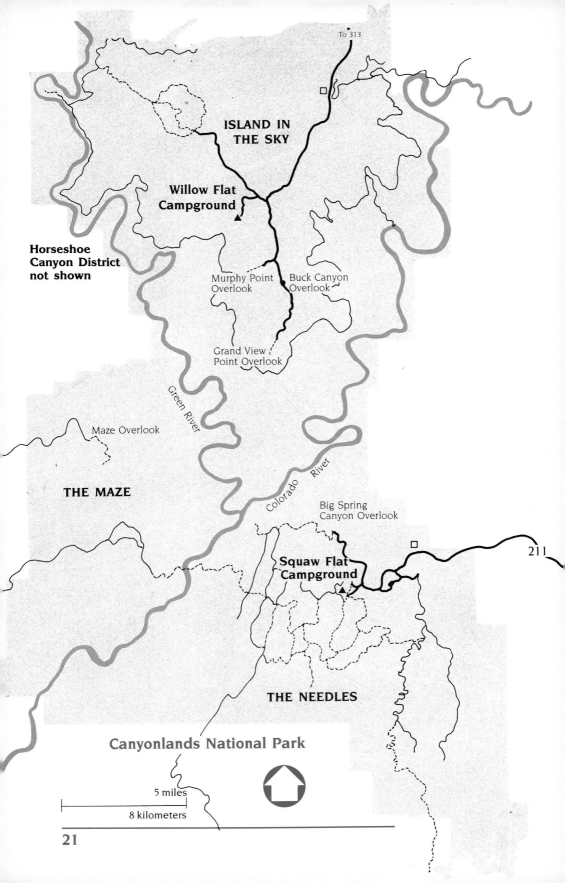

To 313

ISLAND IN
THE SKY

Willow Flat
Campground

Horseshoe
Canyon District
not shown

Murphy Point
Overlook

Buck Canyon
Overlook

Grand View
Point Overlook

Green River

Maze Overlook

THE MAZE

Colorado River

Big Spring
Canyon Overlook

Squaw Flat
Campground

211

THE NEEDLES

Canyonlands National Park

5 miles

8 kilometers

The entrance to this District is 15 miles north of Monticello or 40 miles south of Moab at the junction of US 191 and Utah 211. From this junction it is 31 miles on Utah 211 to the Visitor Information Station.

CAMPGROUND

Squaw Flat Campground (elev. 5125') is located about 4 miles from the Park entrance in a juniper tree grove. It has 26 sites (16 in "Campground A" and 10 in "Campground B") and is open all year. Facilities include tables, grills, water (April through September), and pit toilets. The fee is $5 and camping is on a first-come basis. Limit of stay in the campground is 14 days. There are 3 group campsites available in this campground. The fee is $2/person, minimum $20/ group or 10 people, and reservations are required. Wood-gathering is prohibited.

There is a GROUP CAMP located .4 mi. from the end of Cave Spring Road. It is in a cave with an opening suitable for a fire. It has picnic tables. It will facilitate groups to 15. Reservations are required; the fee is $2/person, minimum $20 or 10 people.

HIKING

Self-Guiding Trails

Road Side Ruin: 0.3mi/0.5km; easy; trailhead: on main Park road just west of Ranger Station. The trail explores Indian granary.

Cave Spring Trail: 0.6mi/1.0km; easy; trailhead: 1.7mi/2.7km off main Park road on the Salt Creek turn-off.

Pothole Point: 0.6mi/1.0km; easy; trailhead: on main Park road approximately 1.0mi/1.6km from the end of the Big Spring Canyon Overlook Road.

From Campground A Trailhead: to CAMPGROUND B .3mi/.5km; to LOST CANYON 2.6mi/4.2km; to PEEKABOO SPRINGS 5.4mi/8.7km; to SQUAW FLAT LOOP TRAIL 7.8mi/12.6km; to DRUID ARCH 8.3mi/13.4km.

From Campground B Trailhead: to CAMPGROUND A .3mi/.5km; to CHESLER PARK 4.9mi/7.9km; to DRUID ARCH 7.4mi/11.9km; to SQUAW FLAT LOOP TRAIL 7.8mi/12.6km.

From Elephant Hill: (located at the end of a 3 mi. dirt road): to CHESLER PARK 2.9mi/4.7km; to SQUAW FLAT CAMPGROUND 5.0mi/8.0km; to DRUID ARCH 5.4mi/8.7km. From the trailhead a rugged four-wheel-drive road continues to RIVER CONFLUENCE* 9mi/14.4km; DEVIL'S KITCHEN CAMP 3.5mi/5.6km; CHESLER PARK 10mi/16km. Parking and picnic tables are at the trailhead.

From Big Spring Canyon Overlook (located at the end of the main Park road): CONFLUENCE* OVERLOOK TRAIL 5.1mi/8.1km.

*Colorado and Green Rivers

ADJACENT FACILITIES

Needles Outpost: .2 mi. on dirt road just north of the Park Boundary; 26 tent sites; 20 sites with hook-ups and showers; no electricity or shade

Newspaper Rock State Park: 12 mi. W of US 191 on Utah 211; open all year; basic camping facilities; very unusual panel of petroglyphs

IN MONTICELLO: Complete commercial facilities including the following campgrounds:

KOA Monticello: 5 mi. E on US 666, ½ mi. N on Co. Rd.; open 5/15–10/15; electricity; sewer; showers; flush toilets; store; laundry; ice; reservations: East Rt., Monticello, UT 84535; 801/587-2884

Mountain View Camper Park: In town; open 5/1–10/1; full hook-ups; showers; flush toilets; laundry; reservations. Box 881, Monticello, UT 84535; 801/587-2974

Westerner Trailer Park: On Hwy. 163, S edge of town; open all year; full hook-ups; showers; flush toilets; laundry; reservations. Box 371, Monticello, UT 84535; 801/587-2762

Dalton Springs USFS *Campground*: 5 mi. W of Monticello on FR 50105; open 5/20–10/25; basic facilities

Buck Board USFS *Campground*: 6.5 mi. W of Monticello on FR 50015; open 5/20–10/25; basic facilities

MAZE DISTRICT

The entrance to this District is through the Hans Flat Ranger Station off Utah 24. The road into Hans Flat and Horseshoe Canyon is two-wheel drive passable most of the year. Horseshoe Canyon is a superb area and very reachable to two-wheel drive. Four-wheel drive is required from the head of the Flint Trail into the Maze country itself. This District is beautifully rugged, being isolated by the Colorado and Green Rivers.

Horseshoe Canyon unit was added to the park in 1971 because of the Indian rock art considered by many to be the most significant in North America. It is accessible to the west rim by two-wheel drive from Utah 24 on a 32-mile dirt road or from Green River, WY on a 45-mile dirt road. Four-wheel access to the canyon is via a 21-mile jeep road that begins at Hans Flat Ranger Station. Hiking distances to the great gallery are approximately 3 miles one-way from the west rim trailhead and 1.5 miles from four-wheel-drive access.

CAMPGROUNDS

There are primitive camps at the Maze overlook as well as along the jeep trails to The Doll House. There is no water. This area averages only 8,000 visitors per year (5% of total Park visitation). Attractions include ancient Indian paintings on the walls of Horseshoe Canyon (see above).

HIKING

Great hiking exists throughout the Maze in sandy canyon bottoms. Rangers have information on numerous cross-country routes which are rock-cairned. Write the Park Superintendent for detailed information on the hiking.

ADJACENT FACILITIES

Green River, WY: complete commercial facilities
Hanksville, UT: basic (but limited) facilities

BRIEF HISTORY

The Anasazi and Fremont Indians both occupied Canyonlands as early as A.D.1000. Undoubtedly earlier cultures preceded them, but little is known about them. The Anasazi left around A.D.1250 and probably migrated south. The Navajo and Ute followed, using the Park area for hunting.

Early American explorers included trappers, the most notable being Denis Julien, who left his name carved on canyon walls as early as 1836. The first overland explorer of note was Captain John Malcomb in 1859. John Wesley Powell, a Civil War casualty having left him with one arm, made historic trips in 1869 and 1871 conquering the Green and Colorado Rivers. His party mapped the region which established Powell as a brilliant leader and explorer.

Cattle and sheep raising flourished in the Needles District starting in the 1880's. Uranium prospecting followed in the 1950's.

The Park was established on September 12, 1964, primarily through the efforts of former Secretary of the Interior Stewart Udall and former Park Superintendent of Arches National Park Bates Wilson.

AUTHOR'S COMMENTS

Each national park has its own distinct personality. Canyonlands is not a touristy-type park; it is remote and rugged and water is a scarce item. It's hot in the summer and cold in the winter and best visited in the spring or fall. In my opinion, the park is best explored to its fullest by 4-wheel vehicle. For those who are accustomed to the family car or RV travel, the park has initiated an ambitious road-building program. Rafting and hiking are also alternatives for exploration. Hiking trails vary from easy to rugged, primitive wilderness. It is a land of mystery and intrigue whose geological story covers a span of 300 million years.

Capitol Reef

NATIONAL PARK, UTAH

LOCATION:	South central Utah
ACCESS:	Utah 24 from east or west
SEASON:	All year
HOURS:	24 hours/day
ENTRANCE FEES:	$3/vehicle/week (non-paved portion of Scenic Dr. beyond Visitor Center and campground); $1/person all others/week; $9 annual; $25 Golden Eagle
GAS, FOOD & LODGING:	None in Park; available in communities to the west and Hanksville to the east
NEAREST PROPANE:	On Utah 24, 20 mi. W to Bicknell; 30 mi. W to Loa
CAMPGROUNDS:	Three in Park; open year-round; first-come basis; no hook-ups
ADJACENT FACILITIES:	In HANKSVILLE, approximately 40 mi. E of Park Headquarters; in TORREY, approximately 11 mi. W of Park Headquarters; RIM ROCK RANCH: just outside W Entrance to Park with 54 sites, full hook-ups, showers, restaurant
VISITOR CENTER:	Capitol Reef Visitor Center off Utah 24
MUSEUM:	Exhibits in Visitor Center
PICNICKING:	Three areas in Park: 3.5 mi. E of Visitor Center on Utah 24;

.75 mi. from Visitor Center on Scenic Dr.; on Burr Trail in southern part of Park

TOURS:	Ranger-guided walks and hikes; auto caravan guided tours
ACTIVITIES:	Hiking; backpacking (permit required); four-wheeling; interpretive programs
CLIMATE:	Warm in summer; cold in winter; most rain from summer thundershowers
ELEVATION:	3,900 to 8,800 ft.
SIZE:	378 sq. miles
ANNUAL VISITATION:	Approximately one-half million
PETS:	Must be on leash; not permitted on trails or in backcountry
FACILITIES FOR DISABLED:	Visitor Center; restrooms
INFORMATION:	*Supt. Capitol Reef National Park Torrey, UT 84775 801/425-3791*

CAMPGROUNDS

Fruita (elev. 5400') is located 1 mi. S of the Visitor Center and 9 mi. from the eastern entrance to the Park. It has 70 individual sites and 2 group campsites for 20 campers each (reservations required). The campground is open all year. The fee is $5, and campsites are on a first-come basis with a 14-day limit of stay. Facilities include tables and charcoal firestands, water, modern comfort stations, and a dump station. Wood-gathering is prohibited, and ground fires are not allowed. An amphitheater provides a site for evening interpretive programs.

Cedar Mesa (elev. 5600') is located 20 mi. S of Utah 24 on a dirt road. It has 5 sites and is open all year. No fee is charged, and campsites are on a first-come basis with a 14-day limit of stay. The campground has tables and pit toilets but *no water.*

Cathedral (elev. 7000') is located approximately one-half mile E of the Harnet-Caineville Wash Road junction (on Caineville Wash Road). It has 5 sites and is open all year. No fee is charged, and campsites are on a first-come basis with a 14-day limit of stay. The campground has tables and pit toilets but *no water.*

HIKING

Goosenecks: .25mi/.4 km one way ; easy; trailhead: Goosenecks Overlook. The trail offers views of Sulphur Creek Canyon, panoramas, and interesting rock formations along the way.

Chimney Rock: 3.5mi/5.6km round trip; moderate to strenuous; trailhead: Utah 24. Views of Chimney Rock as well as panoramas of the surrounding area are features of this hike.

Hickman Bridge: 1.0mi/1.6km one way; moderate; trailhead: Utah 24. This is a self-guiding nature trail which leads under Hickman Natural Bridge.

Rim Overlook: 2.25mi/3.6km one way; strenuous; trailhead: Hickman Bridge. The trail ascends to the top of thousand-foot cliffs with spectacular views to east, west and south.

Cohab Canyon: 1.75mi/2.8km one way; strenuous to moderate; trailhead: Fruita Campground. This trail climbs to a hidden canyon high above the campground, and short side trails lead to overlooks.

Frying Pan: 3.0mi/4.8km between Cohab & Cassidy trails; strenuous; trailhead: 1-mile mark on Cohab Canyon Trail. This trail links Cohab and Cassidy trails via summit of reef, with many ups and downs over slickrock and canyons.

Cassidy Arch: 1.75mi/2.8km one way; strenuous; trailhead: Grand Wash parking area. The trail ascends steeply from the floor of Grand Wash to high cliffs, ending above and behind Cassidy Arch.

Grand Wash: 2.25mi/3.6km one way; easy; trailhead: Grand Wash parking area. This mostly-level trail goes along the bottom of the Wash with the sheer canyon walls rising close by on either side.

Fremont River: 1.25mi/2.0km one way; very easy to strenuous; trailhead: adjacent to campground amphitheater. The first half mile of this trail is a walk through orchards by the river and is suitable for handicapped. Then it climbs steeply to an overlook of the canyon and valley.

Capitol Gorge: 1.0mi/1.6km one way; easy; trailhead: Capitol Gorge parking area. This trail is similar to Grand Wash Trail but also features prehistoric Indian petroglyphs, Pioneer Register and waterpockets or "tanks".**

Golden Throne: 2.0mi/3.2km one way; strenuous; trailhead: Capitol Gorge parking area. Scenic views abound as this trail climbs from the bottom of Gorge to the top of the cliffs and base of Golden Throne.

**There is a 10-mile unpaved but well-maintained scenic road to Capitol Gorge. It is not recommended for trailers and there is a spot provided for their parking. The end of the road serves as a trailhead for hikes out of the canyon, 2 mi., and the "tanks", .75 mi.

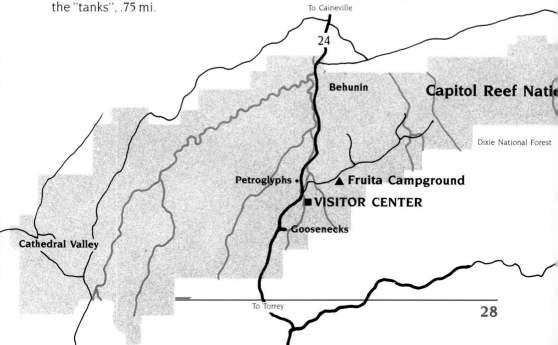

The Fremont Indians were the first people to occupy the area with a highly-developed culture. They abandoned the area around A.D. 1300, leaving behind pictographs and petroglyphs as outstanding examples of their art. They were followed by the southern Paiutes, who were occupying the region when the white man arrived.

This land was originally homesteaded by Mormons in the 1880's. They founded the village of Fruita at the junction of the Fremont River and Sulphur Creek, planting fruit orchards which still remain today. Also standing today is the Fruita school house constructed by residents in 1896.

In the 1920's, Joseph Hickman and Emphraim Pectol, along with other locals, started the political process to make the area a national monument, which occurred August 2, 1937. A major portion of the geographic phenomenon known as the Waterpocket Fold was added when Capitol Reef became a national park December 18, 1971.

The last of the Fruita residents left Capitol Reef by the 1970's as the Park Service purchased all of the Fruita lands. The orchards are presently owned and managed by the Park Service.

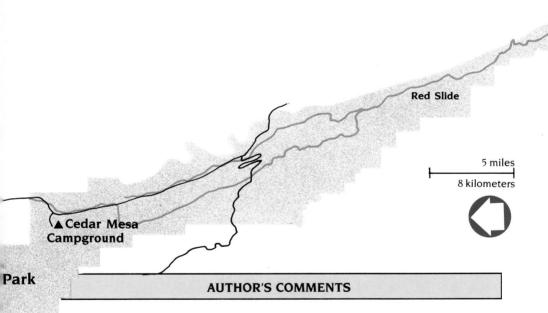

Red Slide

5 miles

8 kilometers

▲ Cedar Mesa
Campground

Park

AUTHOR'S COMMENTS

For the author traveling from Canyonlands to Bryce Canyon National Parks, Capitol Reef is like an oasis in a desert. The campground is located adjacent to a green meadow and an orchard, and, with its sprinkling of shade trees and carpet of lawn, is a welcome contrast to the arid desert that surrounds it. Its location half-way between Canyonlands and Bryce adds to its desirability as a spot to rest and enjoy.

Farming is not what comes to mind in a national park, but here it seems appropriate. And as in Canyonlands National Park, four-wheeling is the best way to explore the entire Park.

Channel Islands

LOCATION: Five islands (Anacapa, Santa Barbara, San Miguel, Santa Rosa and Santa Cruz) offshore So. California between Santa Barbara and San Pedro

ACCESS: To Park Headquarters and Visitor Center from Ventura, Seaward Ave. exit off US 101 (Victoria Ave. exit from south); private, charter or concessioner-operated boat service to islands from Ventura, Santa Barbara or Oxnard (see below for boating and landing information)

SEASON: All year (access to islands subject to weather conditions)

HOURS: Visitor Center 8 a.m. to 5 p.m. daily, extended in summer

ENTRANCE FEE: None

LANDING PERMIT: Required for San Miguel and Santa Rosa Islands (contact Channel Islands Nat'l Park Headquarters 805/644-8262)

GAS, FOOD & LODGING: Cities of Ventura, Santa Barbara and Oxnard

CAMPGROUNDS: Primitive camping on Santa Barbara Island and E. Anacapa Island; free permit required (see below)

VISITOR CENTERS: Island information and displays at Ventura Harbor, E. Anacapa Island and Santa Barbara Island

MUSEUM: Anacapa Island Museum

PICNICKING: Santa Barbara Island and Anacapa Island (restrooms but no fresh water)

TOURS: NPS Ranger-guided walks on Anacapa daily in summer; Nature Conservancy trips monthly to Santa Cruz Island all year for general public and organized groups (805/962-1111); Island transportation and Whale Watch trips January through March with Island Packers Co. (805/642-1393)

ACTIVITIES: Hiking; swimming; scuba diving; snorkeling; nature observation; photography; fishing (California state license required); interpretive programs

CLIMATE: Temperate; some fog and strong winds

ELEVATION: Sea level to 2450 feet

SIZE: 196 sq. mi. on islands and 195 sq. mi. of submerged lands

ANNUAL VISITATION: Approximately one-third million

PETS: Not allowed

FACILITIES FOR DISABLED: Park Headquarters and Visitor Center

INFORMATION: Supt. Channel Islands National Park
1901 Spinnaker Drive
Ventura, CA 93001
805/644-8262   Park Emergency: 911

CAMPING

Camping is allowed only in designated areas on Santa Barbara Island and E. Anacapa Island. It is restricted to 30 persons per island, 14 days per person, and is by free permit only. For information/reservation application, contact National Park Service, Channel Islands National Park, 1901 Spinnaker Dr., Ventura, CA 93001; 805/644-8262. Reservations may not be made more than 60 days in advance.

Campgrounds are equipped with tables, pit toilets and grills. Campers must provide water and fuel. During summer months and adverse weather conditions, open fires are prohibited, so campers must provide small cooking stove.

It is advisable to keep camping equipment as light as possible, as accessibility to camping areas is via about 150 steps plus ¼ mile on Anacapa and a steep trail on Santa Barbara Island.

TRANSPORTATION AND LANDING

Landing Permits

East Anacapa: No landing permit required

West Anacapa: Contact Park Headquarters (permit not required for landing at Frenchy's Cove)

Santa Rosa: Contact Park Headquarters

San Miguel: Contact Park Headquarters

Photo: National Park Service

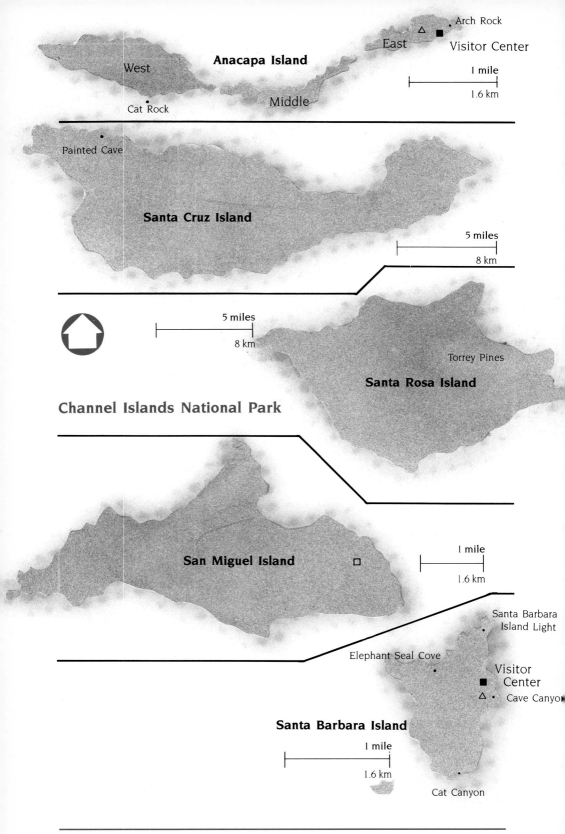

Anacapa Island
West
Middle
East
Cat Rock
Arch Rock
Visitor Center
1 mile
1.6 km

Painted Cave
Santa Cruz Island
5 miles
8 km

5 miles
8 km

Torrey Pines
Santa Rosa Island

Channel Islands National Park

San Miguel Island
1 mile
1.6 km

Santa Barbara
Island Light
Elephant Seal Cove
Visitor
Center
Cave Canyon

Santa Barbara Island
1 mile
1.6 km
Cat Canyon

Santa Cruz:

For east of property line between Chinese Harbor and Sandstone Point, contact Mr. Pier Gherini, 114 State Street #230, Santa Barbara, CA 93101; 805/966-4155 or Mr. Francis Gherini, 162 South A Street, Oxnard, CA 93030; 805/483-8022. Requests must be in writing; enclose self-addressed stamped envelope.

For west of property line between Chinese Harbor and Sandstone Point, contact the Santa Cruz Island Co., 515 South Flower Street, Los Angeles, CA 90071; 213/485-9208. A fee is charged for this permit.

Commercial Boat Service

For Park concessioner-operated boat service, contact Island Packers Company, P.O. Box 993, Ventura, CA 93002; 805/642-1393. Reservations should be made in advance of trip date.

For list of commercial boat carriers, contact Park Headquarters.

Using Your Boat

Boaters must be familiar with changing and sometimes hazardous conditions in the Santa Barbara Channel. Reference should be made to U.S. Coast and Geodetic Survey Charts 18720, 18729 and 18756. Good cruising guides are available at Visitor Center.

Going ashore on Anacapa, San Miguel, Santa Rosa or Santa Barbara Islands requires a skiff, raft or small boat.

It is recommended that campers use commercial boat service, as anchored boats should not be left unattended.

HIKING

Anacapa Island

East Anacapa Island Nature Trail: 1.5mi/2.4km loop; trailhead: Anacapa Island Museum. This trail offers many interesting observation points and an excellent opportunity to view island wildflowers, wildlife and plant life.

Santa Barbara Island

Canyon View Nature Trail: .25mi/.40km loop; 30 minutes; trailhead: Ranger Station near Landing Cove. Superb ocean views, birdwatching and a small island canyon are some features of this pleasant trail.

Arch Point Loop Trail, Elephant Seal Cove Trail and Signal Peak Loop Trail combine to offer 5 more miles of trail for observing seals and sea lions, sea gull rookeries, and unique plant communities.

San Miguel Island

San Miguel Trail: 14mi/22.4km round trip; trailhead: Ranger Station overlooking Cuyler Harbor. This is a Ranger-guided tour requiring a landing permit (no self-guided tours).

BRIEF HISTORY

The first inhabitants of Channel Islands were the Chumash Indians, whose sustenance was trading the islands' natural resources and their excellent crafts with mainland Indians. They remained in their villages on the islands until the early 1800's, when they were removed to mainland missions.

The first European on the islands was Juan Rodriquez Cabrillo, a navigator in service to Spain, in 1542. And in 1793, the present names of the Islands were fixed on nautical charts by English Captain George Vancouver.

Sea otter, seals and sea lions in the islands' coves and on shorelines were hunted nearly to extinction by Russian, British and American fur traders in the late 1700's and early 1800's. Ranching then became the economic mainstay of the islands, and by the mid- to late-1800's, sheep, cattle, honey, olives and wine were being supplied to the mainland by island ranches.

The U.S. Coast Guard (then the U.S. Lighthouse Service) began its stay on Anacapa Island in early 1900, and the U.S. Navy took over San Miguel Island just before World War II. Evidence of military use of the islands as part of our coastal defense during World War II is still in evidence today.

Efforts to help preserve the islands began in 1938 when Santa Barbara and Anacapa Islands were proclaimed Channel Islands National Monument by President Franklin D. Roosevelt. In 1976 an agreement between the National Park Service and U.S. Navy permitted supervised visitation of San Miguel Island. In 1978 the Santa Cruz Island Co. and the Nature Conservancy formed a conservation partnership providing for continued protection, research and educational use of most of Santa Cruz Island. And in 1980, the five islands and the waters one nautical mile around each island became our 40th National Park. Channel Islands National Park is part of the International Man and the Biosphere program today, an effort aimed at conserving genetic diversity and an environmental baseline for research and monitoring throughout the world.

AUTHOR'S COMMENTS

A boat trip to this Park's islands offers RV drivers a pleasant respite from the crowded roads and highways and their unending search for propane or a dump station.

Channel Islands National Park has recently acquired Santa Rosa Island, which is a major expansion of the Park.

Photo: National Park Service

Crater Lake

LOCATION: Southwestern Oregon

ACCESS: Oregon 62 from west and south; Oregon 138 from north

SEASON: Year round on south access road; north entrance and Rim Drive closed mid-October to July

HOURS: Summer, 24 hours/day; winter, til dusk

ENTRANCE FEES: $5/vehicle/week; $2/person all others/week; $15 annual; $25 Golden Eagle

FOOD: Rim Village (restaurant, cafeteria, deli, fountain and store)

GAS: Near Park Headquarters, from Memorial Day to October

NEAREST PROPANE: Fort Klamath

LODGING: **Crater Lake Lodge:** In Rim Village, 6 mi. from Annie Spring Entrance Station; open early June to early Sept.; 79 lodge rooms and 4 cabins, some with private baths; no cooking facilities; dining room; cocktail lounge; cafeteria; gift shop; reservations: Crater Lake, OR 97604, 503/549-2511

CAMPGROUNDS: 198 sites at Mazama Campground for tents or trailers; 12 tent-only sites at Lost Creek; no hook-ups

ADJACENT FACILITIES: Several RV parks and campgrounds (see below)

VISITOR CENTERS: Rim Village Visitor Center (open daily summer and fall); William G. Steel Center, near Park Headquarters (open daily year round)

MUSEUMS: Displays at Visitor Center, Sinnott Memorial and Steel Center

PICNICKING: Designated sites around the Lake and throughout the Park

GIFT SHOP: Rim Village

TOURS: Boat tours; bus tours (503/549-2511); ranger-led hikes

ACTIVITIES: Hiking; fishing; interpretive programs; cross-country skiing; backcountry camping and hiking (permit required); snowmobiling; scenic boat tours

CLIMATE: Warm days and cold nights in summer (and unpredictable); 8 months of snow

ELEVATION: 4,405 to 8,926 ft.

SIZE: 286 sq. miles

ANNUAL VISITATION: Approximately one-half million

PETS: Must be on leash; not permitted on trails or in buildings

FACILITIES FOR DISABLED: Most facilities and some restrooms; scripts of some interpretative talks available for hearing impaired

INFORMATION: Supt. Crater Lake National Park
P.O. Box 7   Crater Lake, OR 97604
503/594-2211   Park Emergency: 911 or 800/452-5021

CAMPGROUNDS

Mazama: (elev. 6000') is located .3 miles from the Annie Spring Entrance Station (south) in a spacious, wooded area. It has 198 sites, some of which can accommodate RV's up to 40 ft. long, and is open, depending on snow conditions, from July to October. The campground usually fills by 5 p.m. to 7 p.m. from mid-July through Labor Day. Facilities include tables and grills, modern comfort stations, water, an amphitheater, and a sanitary dump station. The fee is $7 per night with a limit of stay of 14 days, and campsites are on a first-come basis. Wood is for sale at the campground, and down and dead wood may be gathered in certain areas. The campground has handicapped access.

Lost Creek: (elev. 5972') is located on Pinnacles Road 3 miles from the junction with Rim Road. It has 12 sites for tents or small trailers, and is open, depending on snow conditions, from mid-July to October. Facilities include tables and grills, pit toilets, and water. There is no fee, and limit of stay is 14 days. The campground is usually filled.

ADJACENT FACILITIES

Crater Lake RV Park: 2.5 miles from south entrance in spacious, grassy area with shade and a stream; open 5/15–10/15; full hook-ups; showers; flush toilets; store; laundry; ice; telephones; reservations: Box 485, Ft. Klamath, OR 97626, 503/381-2275

Diamond Lake RV Park: Approximately 10 mi. N of Park, 1 mi. N of junction of Hwys. 230 and 138 on Old Hwy. 138; open 5/1–10/1; full hook-ups; showers; flush toilets; dump station; laundry; reservations: Diamond Lake, OR 97731, 503/793-3318

Fort Creek Resort: 25 mi. S of Park on Hwy. 62; open 5/1–11/1; full hook-ups; showers; flush toilets; laundry; reservations: Box 457, Ft. Klamath, OR 97262, 503/381-2207

Mill Creek USFS Campground: 2 mi. N of Prospect on Hwy. 62, 1 mi. E on FR 30; open 5/25–9/10; information: 503/560-3623

HIKING

There are over 30 trails in Crater Lake National Park ranging in length from less than a mile to the Pacific Crest Trail of approximately 33 miles which bisects the Park from north to south. These trails comprise, in all, over 140 miles. The main thrust of the hiking for most visitors is climbing the various peaks of the caldera surrounding Crater Lake. These trails include the following (all distances and times one way unless otherwise indicated):

Garfield Peak: 1.7mi/2.7km; 1 hour; ascent 1010'; trailhead: Caldera rim E of Crater Lake lodge. This moderately steep trail is usually free of snow by mid-July and offers a spectacular view of Crater Lake from 2,000 ft. above the Lake.

The Watchman: .8mi/1.3km; ½hr.; ascent 456'; trailhead: Watchman Overlook

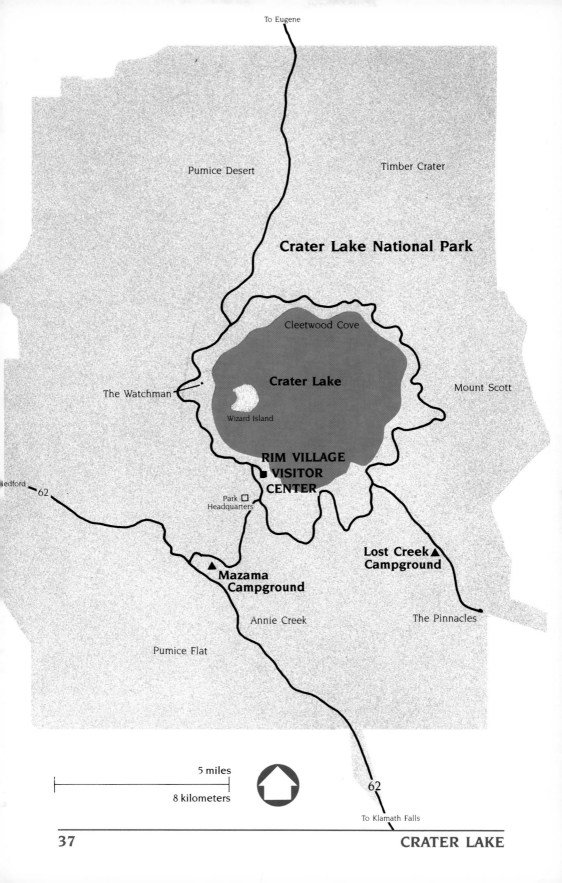

To Eugene

Pumice Desert

Timber Crater

Crater Lake National Park

Cleetwood Cove

The Watchman

Crater Lake

Mount Scott

Wizard Island

RIM VILLAGE VISITOR CENTER

edford

62

Park ☐
Headquarters

Lost Creek ▲ Campground

▲ **Mazama Campground**

Annie Creek

The Pinnacles

Pumice Flat

5 miles

8 kilometers

62

To Klamath Falls

CRATER LAKE

3.7mi/5.9km NW of Rim Village. This moderately steep trail is usually free of snow by late July or August. Views of Wizard Island and Crater Lake are impressive.

Mt. Scott: 2.5mi/4.0km; 1–1.5 hrs; ascent 1476'; trailhead: Rim Drive pullout 16.8/26.9km clockwise from Rim Village. This trail is moderately steep and climbs to the Park's highest point. The summit provides outstanding views in all directions.

Godfrey Glen: 1.0mi/1.6km loop; ½–1 hr; ascent 50'; trailhead: Parking area on Park Rd. 2.4mi/3.8km S of Park Headquarters. This almost level loop trail passes through a magnificent forest of mountain hemlock and red fir (silvertip) with views of Annie Creek Canyon.

Annie Creek Canyon: 1.7mi/2.7km loop 1–1½ hrs; descent 200'; trailhead: behind Mazama Campground amphitheater between loops D & E; descent: 200 vertical ft. This trail travels to the bottom of Annie Creek Canyon. Wildflowers are profuse along Annie Creek and wildlife is common.

Cleetwood Cove: Only trail to the Lake 1.1mi/1.8km; ½ hr.; descent 675'; trailhead: Parking area on Rim Dr. 4.5mi/7.2km E of North Rim Road junction. This steep trail provides access to the tour boats. The boats have a regular schedule for a two-hour Lake tour. The tours are operated by the concessioner but are ranger- guided.

*For detailed information on hiking trails, we recommend *Crater Lake National Park Trails* by Constance M. Toops, available at the Visitor Centers.

HISTORY

Crater Lake was discovered by white men in 1853 by a party of prospectors, including John Wesley Hillman, looking for the Lost Cabin Gold Mine. In 1886 a

U.S. Geological Survey party under command of Captain Clarence E. Dutton determined the Lake to be 1996 feet deep. The official depth, as determined by sonar in 1959, is 1932 feet, thus making it the deepest lake in America and the 7th deepest in the world.

William Gladstone Steel lobbied for seventeen years for the creation of Crater Lake National Park. His efforts were culminated on May 22, 1902, when Theodore "Teddy" Roosevelt signed the Bill into law.

Crater Lake was formed in recent times, geologically speaking—some 6,800 years ago. This occurred when a 12,000 foot composite volcano, Mt. Mazama, collapsed after a series of violent eruptions emptied its interior. Eventually the so-called "crater" sealed itself, and the Lake was formed by the melting snows and rain and has stabilized itself at its current level. Wizard Island was formed by another eruption at a later date.

AUTHOR'S COMMENTS

The indigo blue lake may be viewed by auto along Rim Drive or by climbing trails to its surrounding peaks.

During winter, the Park receives up to 50 feet of snow. The south and west entrances are kept open, as well as the road to Rim Village. However, during heavy snow storms the roads may be temporarily closed. The north entrance and Rim Road are closed in winter.

There is no private boating on Crater Lake. The water temperature is 50–60 degrees, so not conducive to swimming. Two-hour boat rides are available to Wizard Island, but I would not recommend the tour if weather is threatening, as boats are open.

An added bonus in visiting Crater Lake National Park is seeing the beautiful forest, primarily of mountain hemlock and red fir, which surrounds the lake. It's seldom mentioned, but it's outstanding.

CRATER LAKE

Glacier

"Waterton/Glacier International Peace Park"

N A T I O N A L   P A R K,   M O N T A N A

LOCATION:	Northwestern Montana
ACCESS:	From United States, U.S. 2 and 89; from Canada, Hwys. 2, 5 or 6
SEASON:	Open all year; only road open during winter is 10-mile stretch of Going-to-the-Sun Road from West Glacier to head of Lake McDonald
HOURS:	24 hours/day
ENTRANCE FEES:	$5/vehicle/week; $2/person all others/week; $15 annual; $25 Golden Eagle
FOOD & GAS:	Numerous facilities throughout Park and in adjacent areas
NEAREST PROPANE:	St. Mary; KOA near west entrance; East Glacier
LODGING:	Numerous facilities throughout Park (see below)
CAMPGROUNDS:	15 campgrounds (8 accessible by paved road); group campsites; 208 backcountry sites in 62 campgrounds (permit required)
ADJACENT FACILITIES:	Numerous commercial facilities in West Glacier and St. Mary; see Adjacent Facilities section below for campground information
VISITOR CENTERS:	Glacier Park Headquarters; Apgar Visitor Center (late May

GLACIER

through mid-Dec., weekends in winter); St. Mary Visitor Center (late May to mid-Oct.); Logan Pass Visitor Center (mid-June to mid-Sept.); Many Glacier Ranger Station; Two Medicine Ranger Station

MUSEUM: Exhibits in all Visitor Centers

PICNICKING: At Apgar, Avalanche, Bowman Lake, Many Glacier, Rising Sun, Sprague Creek and Two Medicine Campgrounds

GIFT SHOPS: Lake McDonald, Many Glacier, Rising Sun, Two Medicine, Agpar and Glacier Park Lodge areas

TOURS: Naturalist-led strolls and hikes; boat tours; horseback trail rides; wilderness camping; raft/hike trips

ACTIVITIES: Hiking; boating; fishing; golfing; backpacking; cross-country skiing; photography; bicycling; interpretive programs

CLIMATE: Warm days, cool nights in summer; snow and cold in winter

ELEVATION: 3,154 to 10,466 ft.

SIZE: 1,600 sq. miles (over 1 million acres)

ANNUAL VISITATION: Almost two million

PETS: Must be on leash; not permitted on trails, in backcountry or in public buildings

FACILITIES FOR DISABLED: For the hearing impaired, some texts and written descriptions of talks and walks; for the visually impaired, a tape recording of Park brochure at Apgar and St. Mary Visitor Centers; for the mobility impaired, Apgar and St. Mary Visitor Centers, The Trail of the Cedars and other Park areas

INFORMATION: *Supt. Glacier National Park*
West Glacier, MT 59936
406/888-5441
Park Emergency: West Side:888-5407; St. Mary (E. Side): 732-4401

CAMPGROUNDS

• All campgrounds are on a first-come basis.
• Camping limit of stay in auto campgrounds is 7 days in July and August and 14 days per year.
• Dead and down firewood outside campgrounds may be gathered; firewood is for sale at concessioner facilities near several campgrounds.
• Each campsite is provided with a table and fire grate.
• Trailer space (varying limits of from 18' to 35') is provided at all campgrounds except Sprague Creek (no towed units).
• The following campgrounds have paved access roads, flush toilets and water, and a daily fee of $6: Apgar, Avalanche, Fish Creek, Many Glacier, Rising Sun, St. Mary, Two Medicine and Sprague Creek.
• The following campgrounds have unimproved road access, pit toilets and water, and a daily fee of $4: Bowman Lake, Cut Bank, Kintla Lake, Logging Creek and Quartz Creek.
• Bowman Creek and River Campgrounds have unimproved road access and pit

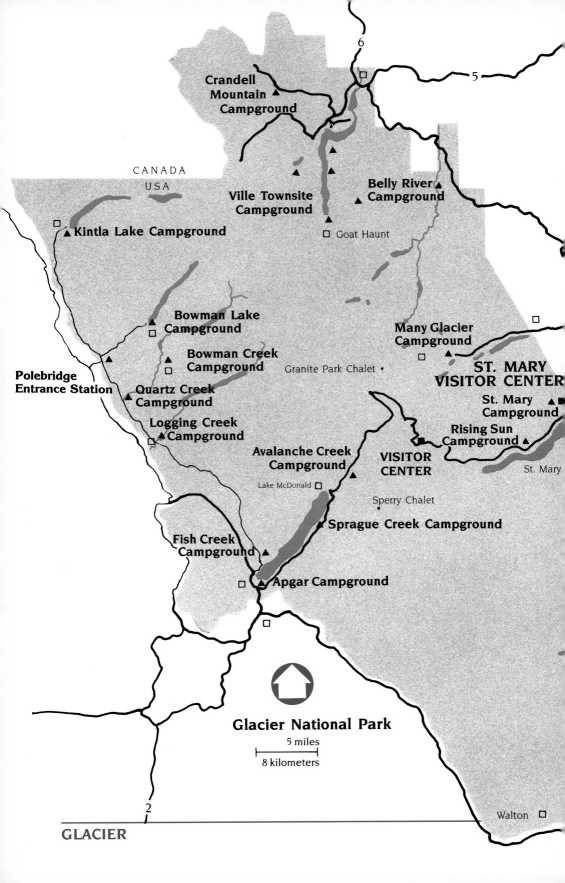

6

5

Crandell Mountain Campground ▲

CANADA

USA

Ville Townsite Campground ▲

Belly River Campground ▲

□ **Kintla Lake Campground** ▲

□ Goat Haunt

Bowman Lake Campground ▲
□

Many Glacier Campground ▲
□

□

Bowman Creek Campground ▲
□

Granite Park Chalet •

ST. MARY VISITOR CENTER

Polebridge Entrance Station
▲

Quartz Creek Campground ▲

St. Mary Campground ▲ ■

Logging Creek Campground ▲
□

Rising Sun Campground ▲

Avalanche Creek Campground ▲

VISITOR CENTER

St. Mary

Lake McDonald □

Sperry Chalet •

Fish Creek Campground ▲

Sprague Creek Campground ▲

□ **Apgar Campground** ▲

□

⌂

Glacier National Park

5 miles

8 kilometers

2

Walton □

GLACIER

toilets; there is no water and no fee.
- Large vehicles are not recommended on unimproved access roads.
- Some campgrounds have no water in winter (see below).
- All campgrounds have fishing available (non-fee permit required) and many have boating access.
- Campstores are located at Apgar, Lake McDonald, Rising Sun, Many Glacier, and Two Medicine.

Apgar (elev. 3173') is located 2 mi. N of W Entrance in a heavily wooded area. The campground has 196 individual sites (8 will accommodate 35' vehicles), 10 group sites, and is open all year but has no water 10/1–5/1. Facilities include a dump station, amphitheater, picnic area, boat access, cafe, store, nearby horseback riding, and phones. The campground has handicapped access.

Avalanche (elev. 3400') is located 10 mi. NE of W Entrance in a heavily wooded area. *This is a hard-sided vehicle campground only*—no tents or tent trailers. It has 87 sites and is open July–Sept. Features include a dump station, amphitheater, picnic area, and ranger station. The campground has handicapped access.

Bowman Creek (elev. 3800') is located near Polebridge Entrance in a ponderosa pine forest adjacent to Bowman Creek. It has 6 sites and is open June–Sept. A store, gas station, and post office are located 2 miles away in Polebridge.

Bowman Lake (elev. 4000')is located 6 mi. E of Polebridge Entrance at the foot of Bowman Lake. It has 48 sites and is open mid-May until closed by snow. There are picnic areas and a ranger station at the campground.

Cut Bank (elev. 4900') is located 4 mi. W of US 89. It has 19 sites and is open June until closed by snow.

Fish Creek (elev. 3200') is located 4 mi. NW of W Entrance in a heavily wooded area adjacent to Lake McDonald. It has 180 sites and is open mid-June to Sept. The campground has a picnic area and handicapped access.

Kintla Lake (elev. 4000') is located 15 mi. N of Polebridge Entrance at the foot of Kintla Lake. It has 19 sites and is open mid-May until closed by snow. Facilities include a ranger station.

Logging Creek (elev. 3437') is located 14 mi. S of Polebridge Entrance. It has 8 sites and is open mid-May until closed by snow.

Many Glacier (elev. 4878') is located 13 mi. W of Babb near Swiftcurrent Lake in a wooded area. *This is a hard-sided vehicle campground only* –no tents or tent trailers. It has 117 sites (13 will accommodate 35' vehicles) and is open June–Sept. Facilities include a dump station, amphitheater, ranger station, picnic area, phone and nearby showers. The campground has handicapped access.

Quartz Creek (elev. 3500') is located 6 mi. S of Polebridge Entrance. It has 7 sites and is open July–Sept. It is adjacent to the Quartz Creek Trail trailhead.

Rising Sun (elev. 4500') is located 6 mi. W of St. Mary Entrance in a moderately wooded setting near the shore of St. Mary Lake. It has 83 sites (3 will accommodate 30' vehicles) and is open June–Oct. The campground usually fills by early afternoon during the summer. Facilities include a dump station, amphitheater, picnic area, and nearby showers. A cafe, cabins and gas are available during summer months.

River (North Fork) (elev. 3500') is located 2 mi. N of Polebridge Entrance. It has 7 sites and is open mid-May until closed by snow.

Cut Bank
Camp-
round

Two
Medicine
Campground

2

Sprague Creek (elev. 3200') is located 9 mi. N of West Entrance on the shore of Lake McDonald. It has 25 sites and is open mid-June to Sept. This campground fills up all summer. Facilities include a picnic area, horseback riding and a nearby cafe.

St. Mary Lake (elev. 4500') is located 1 mi. NW of St. Mary Entrance adjacent to St. Mary River. It has 156 sites (5 will accommodate 30' vehicles) and is open all year (no water Oct–May). Facilities include a dump station and nearby cafe. The campground has handicapped access.

Two Medicine (elev. 5100') is located 7 mi W of Mont. 49 at the foot of Two Medicine Lake. It has 99 sites (13 will accommodate 32' vehicles) and is open June until closed by snow. Facilities include a dump station, campstore and picnic area. The campground has handicapped access.

BACKCOUNTRY CAMPING

Backcountry campers must obtain a Backcountry Use Permit. These free permits are available at Ranger Stations and Visitor Centers. Reservations for campground use cannot be made previous to the day before departure time. Limit of stay is 3 days per campground, 6 days maximum per trip. However, this limit may be extended by contacting a Ranger, Visitor Center or Information Center.

There are 62 backcountry campgrounds and varying regulations for each. Check for details when obtaining Backcountry Use Permit.

ACCOMMODATIONS

There are numerous lodges, hotels, inns and cabins in Glacier Park offering spectacular scenic views, special traditions, historic architecture and interest, and a rich variety of atmospheres. Most are open June to mid-September. Facilities include informal dining rooms, cocktail lounges, pools, golf, some housekeeping cabins, and evening entertainment. For reservations/information contact Glacier Park, Inc., Greyhound Tower, Station 5185, Phoenix, AZ 85077; 602/248-2600 (mid-Sept. to mid-May) or Glacier Park Inc., East Glacier, MT 59434; 406/226-5551 (mid-May to mid-Sept.); in Montana, 800/332-9351.

For Apgar Village Lodge, open May through September, telephone 406/888-5484.

There are two high country chalets in Glacier accessible only by hiking or horseback and open July to Labor Day. Overnight accommodations, meals and a la carte food service are provided. For reservations/information contact Belton Chalets, P.O. Box 188, West Glacier, MT 59936; tele. 408/888-5511.

ADJACENT FACILITIES

There are complete commercial facilities including lodges, motels, RV parks, gas stations and laundromats at East and West Glacier and St. Mary.

Listed below are RV parks with full hook-ups, dump stations and showers and U.S. Forest Service campgrounds with basic camping facilities.

East Side of Park

Chewing Blackbones: 7 mi. E of St. Mary on US 89; open mid-May through Labor Day; 102 trailer sites; reservations: Box 437, Babb, MT 59411, 406/732-9995

Johnsons of St. Mary: Rte. 89, .25 mi. N of St. Mary up the hill; open May–Oct.; 60 tent and 52 trailer sites; reservations: Browning, MT 59417, 406/732-5565

KOA Kampground: Rte. 89, 1 mi. NW of St. Mary; open mid-May through Sept; 125 tent and 127 trailer sites; reservations: St. Mary Rt., Browning, MT 59417, 406/732-4422

Chief Mountain: Rte. 89, 4 mi. N of Babb at Chief Mtn. Junction

U.S.F.S.—Summit: 10 mi. W of East Glacier; open mid-June to mid-Sept.; 21 tent and 21 trailer sites

West Side of Park

KOA Kampground: 2.5 mi. W of West Glacier off US 2; open May–Oct; 16 tent and 100 trailer sites; reservations: Bx. 215, W. Glacier, MT 59936, 406/387-5341

Glacier CG: 1 mi. W of West Glacier off US 2; open mid-May to mid-Sept.; 19 tent and 170 trailer sites; reservations: Bx. 447, W. Glacier, MT 59936, 406/387-5689

Sundance: 4 mi. W of West Glacier on US 2

U.S.F.S.—Emery Bay: 9 mi. W, US 2, West Glacier, 7 mi. E on Hungry Horse Res. open June to mid-Sept.; 8 tent and 8 trailer sites

U.S.F.S.—Lion Lake: 10 mi W of West Glacier on U.S. 2, 1.5 mi. E of Hungry Horse

HIKING

Glacier National Park is a hiker's paradise. There are over 700 miles of trails to choose from. Listed below are brief descriptions of a few samplings. All distances are one-way unless specified otherwise. Average hiking time on level terrain is 2 miles per hour.

Lake McDonald Area

Trail of The Cedars: .2mi/.3km; easy; trailhead: 100 yds. N of Avalanche Campground entrance on Going-to-the-Sun Road. This boardwalk self-guiding nature trail eads through a mature forest of cedar with trees estimated to be 500–700 years old. It is suitable for handicapped, with access in Loop A of the Campground.

Avalanche Lake: 2.0mi/3.2km; ascent 500′; trailhead: end of Trail of the Cedars boardwalk. This is an extension of the above trail, following Avalanche Gorge to the Lake. Bear and deer can sometimes be seen on the trail.

Huckleberry Mountain: .6mi/1.0km; easy; trailhead: top of Camas Creek Overlook. This self-guiding nature trail leads through a young forest regenerating after the 1967 forest fire.

Logan Pass Area

Hanging Gardens: 1.5mi/2.4km; ascent 400′; trailhead: behind Visitor Center. The self-guiding nature trail begins gradually along a boardwalk before ascending to a viewing platform at the Hidden Lake overlook. Goats, marmots and bears may be seen along the way.

Highline Trail to Granite Park Chalet: 7.6mi/12.2km; ascent 600'; trailhead: across road from Visitor Center parking lot. This relatively-level trail follows the Continental Divide along the Garden Wall. Grizzly bear, eagles, goats, sheep and marmots may be seen along the way.

St. Mary Area

Sun Point: .7mi/1.2km; trailhead: Sun Point parking lot. This self-guiding nature trail follows the shore of St. Mary Lake to Baring Falls, offering views of the historic site of the old chalets and possibly ouzel birds near the Falls. You may continue on this trail to St. Mary Falls (another 1mi/1.6km) and then Virginia Falls (2mi/3.2km).

St. Mary Falls: .8mi/1.3km/ *Virginia Falls* 1.5mi/2.4km; trailhead: on Going-to-the-Sun Road 10.5 mi. W of St. Mary (or see above). This trail offers wildflowers and forest as it leads to the Falls.

Two Medicine Area

Running Eagle Falls: 400yd/366m; easy; trailhead: 2 mi. E of Ranger Station. This gentle trail leads to a waterfall ever-changing with the seasons.

Appistoki Falls: .5mi/.8km; ascent 300'/*Scenic Point* 3.1mi/4.9km; ascent another 1600'; trailhead: .6 mi. E of Ranger Station at Mt. Henry Scenic Point trail. Views of the prairie and the Two Medicine drainage are some features of this trail.

Goat Haunt Area (Accessible only by trail [7.0mi/11.2km from Waterton Townsite] or boat launch services)

Lake Janet: 3.0mi/4.8km; moderate; trailhead: Ranger Station. This trail follows the trail to Boulder Pass, offering a pleasant forest on its climb. It continues past Lake Janet another 2.2mi/3.5km to Lake Francis.

Rainbow Falls: 1.0mi/1.6km; easy; trailhead: Ranger Station. The trail follows Boulder Pass trail before branching off toward the Falls.

Many Glacier Area

Swiftcurrent Lake: 2.4mi/3.8km loop; trailhead: S end of Many Glacier Hotel or Many Glacier Picnic Area. This self-guiding nature trail teaches about animals, plants, geology and history. Pamphlets are available at the trailheads.

Ptarmigan Falls: 2.5mi/4.0km; ascent 500'/*Ptarmigan Lake* 4.2mi/6.7km; ascent another 1000'; trailhead: far end of Swiftcurrent Inn parking lot. The climb to the Falls is gentle, offering abundant wildflowers along the way. There is then a steady ascent to the Lake, with Ptarmigan Tunnel another mile and 500 ft. climb beyond.

Walton Area

Ole Creek: 1.0mi/1.6km; trailhead: picnic area adjacent to Walton Ranger Station on US 2 near Essex. This trail continues from Ole Creek to Firebrand Pass (another 18.4mi/29.4km).

Scalplock Lookout: 4.4mi/7.2km; ascent 3218'; trailhead: Walton Ranger Station picnic area on US 2 near Essex. This trail affords panoramic views of the southern portion of Glacier Park and the Great Bear Wilderness Area.

BRIEF HISTORY

There is no record of Native Americans using the area for permanent settlements. However, as winter snows melted, it is assumed that hunting parties followed migrating animals in search of food.

The prominent Indian tribe of the region when the first white men arrived around 1800 was the Blackfeet. They were a powerful tribe that dominated most of Montana. Intelligent white men gave them a wide berth. The Blackfeet, however, were not exempt from the scourge of white men's diseases, mainly small pox and whiskey (a disease for some white men and Indians). They were further weakened by the destruction of the buffalo herds upon which their culture was built.

The weakening Blackfeet opened the door for prospectors and fur trappers. However, early strikes of minerals petered out.

In the 1890's the Great Northern Railroad tracks (still present) skirted the southern boundary of the present day Park. Early conservationists succeeded in establishing the Lewis & Clark Forest Reserve in 1897. Further efforts by Lyman Sperry and George Grinnell and the Great Northern Railway to establish the area as a national park reached culmination when the Park was established on May 11, 1910. The Going-to-the-Sun Road, an engineering marvel, was completed in 1933. The Road provided an east-west route throught the heart of the Park.

AUTHOR'S COMMENTS

Glacier National Park is one of those parks that, once seen, you want to come back to. It seems you never have enough film or time to enjoy the Park fully. My words can't really describe it, but perhaps the pictures at least give you an idea of its majestic beauty. Glacier is not easily accessible for most Americans, but regardless of how far out of your way you've traveled to get there, you will feel it was well worth it.

Grand Canyon

LOCATION:	Northwestern Arizona
ACCESS:	South Rim: Arizona 64, US 180 North Rim: Arizona 67
SEASON:	South Rim: All year North Rim: Memorial Day to mid-October
HOURS:	24 hours/day
ENTRANCE FEES:	$5/vehicle/week; $2/person all others/week; $15 annual; $25 Golden Eagle
GAS & FOOD:	In Park and nearby towns
NEAREST PROPANE:	South Rim: Grand Canyon Chevron across from Visitor Center North Rim: Kanab, UT (80 mi. N)
CAMPGROUNDS:	South Rim: 2 campgrounds, closed in winter; concession-run trailer village; reservations necessary during summer North Rim: 82 sites, first-come basis, closed in winter; 10 sites, open all year with limited winter access; 3 hike-in campgrounds below rim; reservations required
LODGING:	Numerous facilities throughout Park; Phantom Ranch below the rim (reservations required) (see below)
ADJACENT FACILITIES:	See below
VISITOR CENTERS:	South Rim: Grand Canyon Village North Rim: at time of writing, temporary information center in Grand Canyon Lodge
MUSEUMS:	Tusayan Museum and Yavapai Geology Museum at South Rim
PICNICKING:	Throughout Park at designated areas
GIFT SHOPS:	Numerous shops in lodging facilities; Watchtower Gift Shop at Desert View
TOURS:	Mule trips; guided backcountry tours; bus tours; commercial river tours; horse trips; helicopter and plane tours; Ranger-guided walks
	*NOTE: Reservations required for mule trips. South Rim: Reservations Dept., Grand Canyon National Park Lodges, Grand Canyon, AZ 86023; North Rim: Grand Canyon Trail Rides, Box 1638, Cedar City, UT 84720
ACTIVITIES:	Hiking; fishing (18 mi. round trip hike); biking; rafting; interpretive programs
CLIMATE:	North Rim can be cool and wet; South Rim dry; extreme heat on Canyon floor; rims get snow in winter
ELEVATION:	1,200 to 9,165 ft.
SIZE:	1,100 sq. miles
ANNUAL VISITATION:	Near three million

PETS: Must be on leash; not permitted on trails; kennel available

FACILITIES FOR DISABLED: Available throughout Park; specify needs when making reservations

INFORMATION: *Supt. Grand Canyon National Park*
Box 129 Grand Canyon, AZ 86023
602/638-2411 or 602/638-7888
Park Emergency: 638-2477 or 638-7888

*NOTE: Grand Canyon National Park is on Rocky Mountain *Standard* Time year-round.

CAMPGROUNDS

North Rim (elev. 8400') is located 13 miles south of the north entrance to the Park in a spacious, wooded area. It has 82 individual sites (some suitable for large trailers), 1 group site, and is open mid-May to mid-October. (Group Reservations: North Rim, Grand Canyon, AZ 86023). Facilities include modern comfort stations with flush toilets, water, tables and grills, dump station, store, laundromat, service station, telephone and showers. The fee is $6 per night with a 7-day limit of stay. Campsites are on a first-come basis and usually fill by noon or earlier in summer months.

*NOTE: There is an information center at the junction of Hwys. 89A and 67 where travelers can check on available space in this campground.

Tuweep (elev. 4000') is located at Toroweap Point. It has 10 sites and is open all year, though you probably need a 4x4 to get there in winter. (The campground is 50 miles out on a dirt road which may be impassable after rain). There is no fee, and campsites are on a first-come basis with a 14-day limit of stay. Facilities include pit toilets and water.

*Wood-gathering is not allowed in the Park.

Hike-in Campgrounds

BRIGHT ANGEL is at Phantom Ranch; COTTONWOOD is on the North Kaibab Trail (North Rim); INDIAN GARDENS is on the Bright Angel Trail (South Rim). Permits for overnight camping under the rim are required and advance reservations are advised: Backcountry Reservations Office, Box 129, Grand Canyon, AZ 86023. Campers arriving without reservations should check at the Backcountry Offices for cancellations or openings. Camping is limited to 2 days and there is no fee. Facilities include toilets, water, and picnic tables. No wood or charcoal fires are allowed. Camping under the rim must be in these designated campgrounds and must be reached via designated trails.

ACCOMMODATIONS

Grand Canyon North Rim Lodge: Historic lodge built in 1928; 40 motel units and 163 log cabins (no cooking facilities); dining room; saloon; cafeteria; post office; gift shop; visitor information headquarters; reservations: TW Services, Inc., P.O. Box 400, Cedar City, UT 84720; 801/586-7686

Phantom Ranch: 11 cabins and 4 bunkhouses with bathroom facilities; air-conditioning; snack bar and dining hall; advance reservations (6 months) for mule trip from South Rim to Ranch: Grand Canyon National Park Lodges, Grand Canyon, AZ 86023; 602/638-2401

ADJACENT FACILITIES

North Rim Country Store: 5 mi. N of Park boundary; gas; food; hiking supplies

Kaibab Lodge: 5 mi. N of Park boundary; reservations: 602/638-2389

Demotte Forest Service Campground: .2 mi. off Hwy. 67, 5 miles outside North Rim Entrance Station; 20 trailer and 20 tent sites; open mid-May to October; basic facilities; near store, cafe & ice

Jacob Lake Lodge: 30 mi. N of Park Boundary; reservations: 602/643-7232

Jacob Lake Forest Service Campground: At junction of Hwys. 89A and 67 (30 mi. from North Rim Entrance Station); 48 trailer and 48 tent sites; open mid-May to October; basic facilities; near store, cafe & ice

Jacob Lake RV Camp: ¼ mi. south of Jacob Lake on Hwy. 67; 75 trailer and 50 tent sites; open mid-May to Nov.; full hook-ups; dump station; near store, cafe & ice; reservations: Jacob Lake, AZ 86022

HIKING

North Kaibab Trail: 14.2mi/22.8km one way to Colorado River; trailhead: off main Park road approximately 2mi/3.2km north of Lodge. This is the only maintained trail from the North Rim to the Colorado River and is open only from mid-May to mid-November because of heavy snowfall. The trail descends from elevation 8241 ft. to 2400 ft. Water is available at the junction of Roaring Springs Canyon and Bright Angel Creek (4.7 mi.). Cottonwood Campground is 6.8mi/11km from the trailhead and Bright Angel Campground/Phantom Ranch is 7.3mi/11.7km further. This trail may be taken for the following round-trip day hikes: to Coconino Overlook 1.4mi/2.2km; to Supai Tunnel 3.6mi/5.8km; to Redwall Bridge 5.4mi/8.5km; to Needles Eye 7.0mi/11.2km; to Roaring Springs 10.0mi/16.0km.

*NOTE: The easiest way to hike from rim to rim of the Grand Canyon is to start at the North Kaibab Trail, as the South Rim is 1200 ft. lower in elevation. Arrangements can be made for a 20-minute shuttle flight back to the North Rim from the South Rim.

Bright Angel Point Trail: .5mi/.8km; easy; trailhead: log shelter in Lodge parking lot or east patio behind Lodge. This is a "must" hike, and self-guiding nature trail pamphlets are available. It offers spectacular views of the Canyon and is an excellent place to photograph the sunrise. Roaring Springs can be heard "roaring" from this trail.

Transept Trail: 1.5mi/2.4km one way from Lodge to campground (or vice versa). This lovely trail follows the Canyon rim through a forest of ponderosa pine, white fir, aspen groves, and wildflowers. It has a few ups and downs, and at a number of points the hiker is treated to views of the Canyon. This trail is best taken in the evening as a round trip hike.

Uncle Jim Trail: 5.0mi/8.0km; 3 hours round trip; trailhead: North Kaibab parking lot. This trail winds through forest to a point overlooking the Canyon and North Kaibab trail switchback.

Widforss Trail: 10.0mi/16.0km; 5 hours round trip; trailhead: take dirt road ¼ mi. south of Cape Royal Road for 1 mile to parking lot.

Ken Patrick Trail: 12.0mi/19.3km; 6 hours one way; trailhead: Point Imperial. This trail is not maintained. It winds through forest along the rim to the North Kaibab parking lot. It is very overgrown and may not be possible to follow

---

Cape Royal Trail: 0.6mi/1.0km; 30 minutes round trip; easy; trailhead: Cape Royal parking lot. This paved, level nature trail provides spectacular views of Angels Window and of the Canyon. In the distance, the Colorado River is in view. There's a feeling of excitement in seeing the force that created the Canyon.

Cliff Springs Trail: 1.0mi/1.6km; 30 minutes one way; trailhead: across the road from Angels Window Overlook (a small pullout on a curve .3mi/.5km north of the end of the road to Cape Royal). This trail descends through a forested area past Small Indian River to Cliff Springs and is in poor condition.

AUTHOR'S COMMENTS

The North Rim, due to its elevation averaging approximately 8500 feet, has a pleasant climate with warm days and cool nights. The Kaibab and Walhalla plateaus have beautiful forest mantles of ponderosa pine, white fir, spruce and aspen. Wildflowers abound. The Park is easily viewed by auto, with paved roads to Cape Royal, Grand Canyon Lodge, and Point Imperial.

SOUTH RIM

CAMPGROUNDS

Mather (elev. 6860') is located in Grand Canyon Village. It has 310 individual sites, 7 group sites, and is closed in winter months. The fee is $6 per night. *Reservations are through Ticketron or the Park* May 15-October and on a first-come

basis before May 15 and after September. The campground has a 7-day limit of stay. Facilities include modern comfort stations, water and a dump station. Showers and laundry facilities are adjacent to the campground, and services in the Village include a store and deli, bank, post office and gas station with propane. The campground is useable for the handicapped.

Desert View (elev. 7400') is located ½ mi. W of E Entrance. It has 50 sites and is open May-October. The fee is $6 per night and campsites are on a first-come basis with a 7-day limit of stay. Facilities include modern comfort stations, a nearby store and gas station.

Trailer Village (elev. 6860') is located in Grand Canyon Village. It has 192 trailer sites and is open all year. The fee is $10 per night for the first two persons, with $1 additional for each additional person over 12 years old. (Reservations: Fred Harvey Corp., 602/638-2401). There is a 7-day limit of stay. Facilities include modern comfort stations, full hook-ups, showers, and a dump station. See Mather for services in Grand Canyon Village.

*Wood-gathering is not allowed in the Park.

Hike-in Campgrounds   SEE NORTH RIM.

ACCOMMODATIONS

Lodge Reservations: Grand Canyon National Park Lodges, Inc., P.O. Box 699, Grand Canyon, AZ 86023; 602-638-2401

Bright Angel Lodge: In Grand Canyon Village on the rim; rooms and cabins; dining room; lounge; fountain; curios

El Tovar Hotel: In center of Grand Canyon Village on the rim; dining room; lounge; curios

Kachina and Thunderbird Lodges: Between Bright Angel and El Tovar; modern accommodations

Maswik Lodge: ¼ mi. from the rim in the Village; rooms and cabins; cafeteria; lounge; curios

Yavapai Lodge: Near Visitor Center ⅔ mi. from rim; closed in winter; cafeteria; lounge; fountain

*All lodges open all year except Yavapai.

ADJACENT FACILITIES

Grand Canyon Camper Village: 4 mi. S of Entrance Station on Hwy. 64; open all year; 250 sites; full hook-ups; dump station; store; cafe; ice; reservations: Box 490, Grand Canyon, AZ 86023; 602/638-2887

USFS C.G. Tex X: 10.6 mi S of Grand Canyon on Hwy. 64, .4 mi. E on FR 7302C; 70 tent & trailer sites; store, cafe, laundry and ice within 3 miles

In Tusayan: 4 mi. S of Entrance Station on Hwy 64; complete commercial facilities; airplane and helicopter rides; lodges; information: Grand Canyon Chamber of Commerce, Box 3007, Grand Canyon, AZ 86023

*Always carry water!

South Rim Nature Trail: 3.5mi/5.6km; 2 hours; easy; trailhead: anywhere between Maricopa Pt. on west rim and Yavapai Museum east of Visitor Center. This is a mostly-paved trail with view of the Canyon. Pamphlets are available.

Bright Angel Trail: 7.8mi/12.5km one way; 4 hour descent; 8 hour ascent; strenuous; descent 4460' to the River; trailhead: just W of Bright Angel Lodge. Rest houses are 1.5mi/2.4km and 3.0mi/4.8km below the Rim, with water available in summer. Indian Gardens is 4.6mi/7.4km with water, tables, toilets, camping, ranger station and shade. This trail is one of the two maintained trails from the South Rim to the River. It is not recommended as a day hike.

South Kaibab Trail: 6.3mi/10.2km; 3-4 hour descent; 6-7 hour ascent; strenuous; trailhead: near Yaki Point. Cedar Ridge is 1.5mi/2.3km with toilet. This trail descends 4800 ft. to the River. It is shorter but steeper than the Bright Angel Trail and not recommended as a day hike.

River Trail: 1.7mi/2.7km; allow 1 hour; easy. This trail follows the Colorado River between Bright Angel and South Kaibab Trails.

Desert View Nature Trail: trailhead: Watchtower or campground. This is a 15 minute walk along the Rim.

Tusayan Ruin Walk: trailhead: off Park road 4 mi. W of Desert View. This 20-minute walk wanders through the homes of pre-historic canyon dwellers.

Grandview Trail: 3.0mi/4.8km one way to Horseshoe Mesa; allow 7 hours round trip; strenuous; trailhead: Grandview Point.

There is evidence of human habitat in the Grand Canyon area dating back approximately 4000 years. The first white man exploration of the Canyon was the Cardenas expedition of 1540. In 1776 a Franciscan padre named Francisco

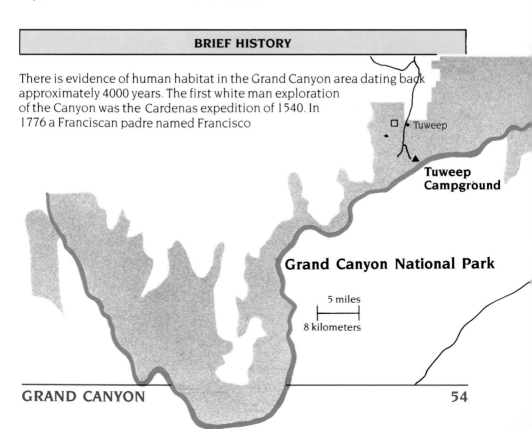

Tuweep

Tuweep
Campground

Grand Canyon National Park

5 miles

8 kilometers

Garcés traveled to the western end of the Canyon. The Joseph C. Ives expedition of 1857-58 sent by the U.S. War Department made the first comprehensive report. John Wesley Powell made spectacular and daring boat trips down the Colorado in 1869 and 1871, winning the one-armed major lasting fame. President Theodore Roosevelt declared the Canyon a National Monument in 1908. It was established as a national park on February 26, 1919, and it has been enlarged several times since.

The geology of the Park is a book by itself. The exposed rocks of the Canyon represent some two billion years of the earth's development. The erosion was mainly caused by the power of the Colorado River.

AUTHOR'S COMMENTS

The Colorado River basically bisects the Park in half. Grand Canyon National Park seems to be two separate parks, a North Rim and a South Rim. Only a 20-minute airplane ride separates the Rims of each. But it's also a 5-hour drive and/or a strenuous hike of several days from one Rim to the other.

The North Rim is closed in the winter due to heavy snow. (It averages around 8500 ft. in elevation.) The South Rim is open all year, and its elevation averages 1000 or more feet less than the North Rim. The higher elevation of the North Rim provides a more beautiful forest mantle, and North Rim has lesser visitation. The South Rim has, in my opinion, more spectacular views of the Canyon and an easier access to the Colorado River.

Be it North or South Rim, Grand Canyon National Park is one of the world's great spectacles. The naked eye, much less a camera, has difficulty capturing the awesome enormity of "The Canyon". Nearly three million people from all over the world visit it every year, and you won't be disappointed if you do.

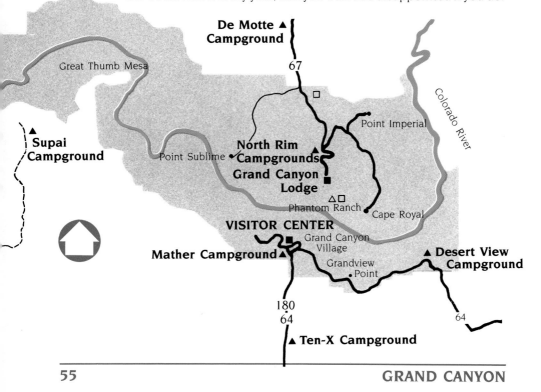

Grand Teton

N A T I O N A L   P A R K ,   W Y O M I N G

LOCATION:	Northwest Wyoming
ACCESS:	Hwy. 89-191-287 from north; Hwy. 26-287 from east; Hwy. 26-89-189-191 from south
SEASON:	All year; the Teton Park Road is plowed north from Moose to Cottonwood Creek turnout parking area, and 89-191 is plowed from Jackson north to the Flagg Ranch; all other roads closed in winter
HOURS:	24 hours/day
ENTRANCE FEES:	$5/vehicle/week (includes admission to Yellowstone); $2/person all others/week; $15 annual; $25 Golden Eagle
FOOD:	Colter Bay; Jackson Lake Lodge; Jenny Lake; Moose; Signal Mountain; Flagg Ranch Village (John D. Rockefeller, Jr. Memorial Parkway) (All summer only except year-round at Moose)
GAS:	Colter Bay; Jackson Lake Lodge; Moose; Signal Mountain; Flagg Ranch Village (All summer only except year-round at Moose)
NEAREST PROPANE:	Colter Bay; Jackson
CAMPGROUNDS:	6 campgrounds; 2 trailer villages with hook-ups, including Flagg Ranch (see Campgrounds section for reservation information); tents only at Jenny Lake; group camping at Colter Bay and Gros Ventre
LODGING:	Colter Bay; Jackson Lake Lodge; Jenny Lake; Moose; Signal Mountain; Flagg Ranch Village (see Accommodations section for reservation information)
ADJACENT FACILITIES:	In *Jackson*, WY, 12 mi. S of Moose Park Headquarters on Hwy. 26-89-191: complete commercial facilities including hotels, motels, restaurants, campgrounds; information: Jackson Hole Chamber of Commerce, Box E, Jackson, WY 83001, 307/733-3316. *Forest Service campgrounds* (E of Kelly on FR 30015): Atherton Creek 7.3 mi., Red Hills 12.8 mi., and Crystal Creek 13.1 mi.; also Trail Creek 5.6 mi. E of Victor on Hwy. 33, .3 mi. S on Hwy. 22.
VISITOR CENTERS:	Colter Bay and Moose
MUSEUM:	Colter Bay Visitor Center—Indian Arts Museum
PICNICKING:	Colter Bay; Jackson Lake; String Lake; near Signal Mountain
GIFT SHOPS:	Colter Bay; Jackson Lake; Moose; Signal Mountain Lodge; Flagg Ranch
TOURS:	Numerous Ranger-led activities (check at Visitor Centers for information); commercial bus tours

FLOAT TRIPS:	Various commercial, interpretive float trips down Snake River during summer months
FIELD SEMINARS:	Natural history and field ecology courses (some conducted while backpacking in the high country) offered by the Teton Science School, Box 68, Kelly, WY 83011; 307/733-4765
OTHER ACTIVITIES:	Horseback riding; mountaineering (permit required); fishing (license required); boating; windsurfing; swimming; bicycling; cross-country skiing; snowmobiling; interpretive programs
CLIMATE:	Warm, dry summers with cool nights and some afternoon thunderstorms; extreme winter conditions with snow averaging 120 inches and nighttime temperatures commonly 20-40 degrees below zero
ELEVATION:	6,400 to 13,770 ft.
SIZE:	485 sq. miles
ANNUAL VISITATION:	Approximately two million
PETS:	Must be on leash; not permitted on trails, in backcountry, and in public buildings
FACILITIES FOR DISABLED:	Most Park facilities, including visitor centers and museum; some ranger-led activities
INFORMATION:	*Supt. Grand Teton National Park* *P.O. Drawer 170* *Moose, Wyoming 83102* *307/733-2880*

CAMPGROUNDS

• Limit of stay is 14 days at all facilities except 7 days at Jenny Lake.
• Reservations are accepted for concession-operated trailer villages at Colter Bay and Flagg Ranch; all other campgrounds on first-come basis.
• The fee is $7 per night at all campgrounds and $13 to $15 at Colter Bay Trailer Village (full hook-ups).
• All campgrounds have tables, fireplaces and modern comfort stations.
• Group camping ($2/person/night) is by reservation only: Between Jan. 1 and June 1, write to Chief Ranger, Grand Teton Nat'l Park, P.O. Drawer 170, Moose, WY 83012.
• Dead and down firewood may be gathered but is scarce.

Colter Bay is located 9 mi. NW of Moran in a level area of lodgepole pine. The campground has 310 individual sites, 10 group camping sites, and is open approximately 5/24–9/24. A dump station, showers and laundry facilities are available nearby (see below for additional services). The campground usually fills by noon during summer months.

Colter Bay Trailer Village is located 9 mi. NW of Moran in a level area of lodgepole pine. The village has 112 sites and is open approximately 5/24–9/24. This is the only facility in the Park with full hook-ups. The fee is $13 to $15 per night and reservations are recommended: Grand Teton Lodge Company, P.O. Box 240, Moran, WY 83013, 307/733-2811. Showers and laundry facilities are available nearby (see below for additional services).

Colter Bay services and activities: stores, restaurant and bar, lodging, ice, firewood, service station with propane, dump stations, ranger station, amphitheater, visitor center, post office, marina with boat launching, swimming, fishing and horseback riding. (Medical clinic at Jackson Lake Lodge.)

Gros Ventre is located 10 mi. SE of Moose. It has 360 individual sites, 5 group camping sites, and is open approximately 5/10–10/15. The campground has a dump station. Stores, post office, and gas station are located within 2 miles, and fishing is available. This campground is usually the last to fill.

Jenny Lake is located 7 mi. N of Moose adjacent to Jenny Lake. The campground is *open to tents and small camping vehicles only* (no trailers). It has 49 sites and is open approximately 5/24–9/24. Services and activities include a store, climbing school, ranger station, boat launch, horseback riding and fishing. The campground usually fills by 8 a.m.

Lizard Creek is located 17 mi. NW of Moran in a pretty site of lodgepole pine forest and wildflowers adjacent to Jackson Lake. The campground has 60 sites (with some walk-in sites) and is open approximately 6/21–9/10. Swimming, boating and fishing are available. This campground usually fills by 2 p.m.
**NOTE: Until approximately 1990 or 91, boating is temporarily closed at the Lizard Creek Campground. Reconstruction of the dam is requiring a lower level of Jackson Lake.

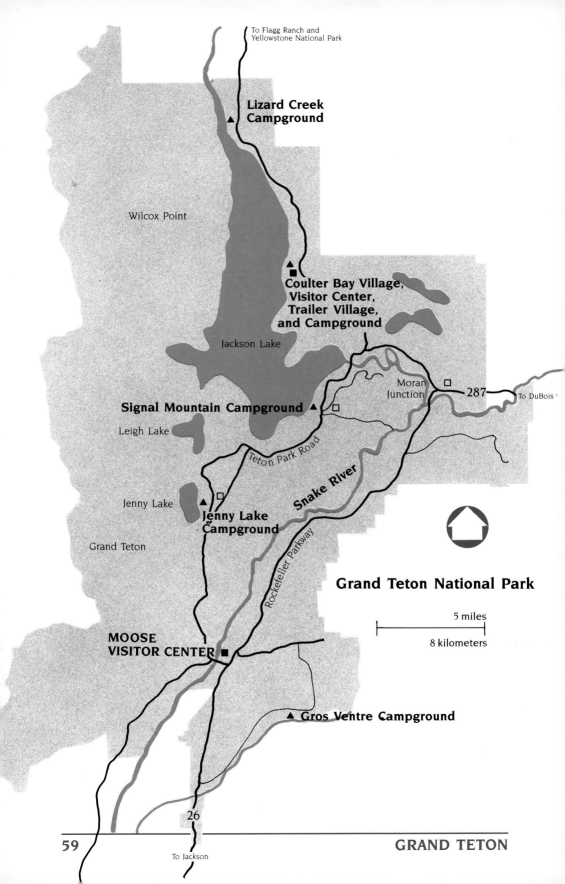

To Flagg Ranch and
Yellowstone National Park

**Lizard Creek
Campground**
▲

Wilcox Point

▲
■
**Coulter Bay Village,
Visitor Center,
Trailer Village,
and Campground**

Jackson Lake

Moran
Junction □ **287**

To DuBois

Signal Mountain Campground ▲ □

Leigh Lake

Teton Park Road

Snake River

Jenny Lake □

Grand Teton

▲
**Jenny Lake
Campground**

Rockefeller Parkway

Grand Teton National Park

5 miles
8 kilometers

**MOOSE
VISITOR CENTER** ■

▲ **Gros Ventre Campground**

26

GRAND TETON

To Jackson

Signal Mountain is located 7 mi. SW of Moran on a forested hillside with beautiful views of the mountains and Jackson Lake. The campground has 86 sites and is open approximately 5/24–9/24. Facilities include an amphitheater and a dump station. Services and activities include a store, restaurant, service station, convenience store, ranger station, lodging, chapel, marina with boat launching, swimming, fishing. The campground usually fills by 10:00 a.m.

Snake River is located in John D. Rockefeller, Jr., Memorial Parkway just north of the Park boundary and is operated by National Park Service. The campground has 24 sites and is open approximately 6/21–9/10. Boating and fishing are available. The campground usually fills by 4 p.m.

Flagg Ranch Trailer Village is located in John D. Rockefeller Jr., Memorial Parkway just north of the Park boundary and is concessioner-operated. The village has 175 sites (130 with hook-ups) and is open approximately 6/1–9/30. Facilities include showers and laundry. The fee is $10 and reservations are advisable: Flagg Ranch, Box 187, Moran, Wyo. 83013, 307/543-2861. Services and activities include a store, fishing and boating.

ACCOMMODATIONS

Jenny Lake Lodge: 30 individual log cabins in a rustic setting; no housekeeping facilities; open June to mid-September; reservations: Grand Teton Lodge Co., Box 240, Moran, WY 83013; 307/733-4647.

Colter Bay Village: 209 log cabins near Jackson Lake; tent cabins also available; open late May to late September; reservations: Grand Teton Lodge Co., Box 240, Moran, WY 83013; (today) 307/543-2828 or 543-2811, (future) 307/543-2855.

Jackson Lake Lodge: 42 hotel rooms and 343 motor lodge rooms; open early June to mid-September; reservations: Grand Teton Lodge Co., Box 240, Moran, WY 83013; (today) 307/543-2811 or (future) 307/543-2855.

Signal Mountain Lodge: Log cabins, lakeside suites, or deluxe family units on the shore of Jackson Lake; open May to October; reservations: Signal Mountain Lodge, Box 50, Moran, WY 83013; 307/543-2831 or 733-5470.

Flagg Ranch Village: Motel units and cabins on the Snake River; cross-country skiing and snowmobile rentals in winter; open 5/15–9/30 & 12/15–3/15; reservations: Flagg Ranch Village, Box 187, Moran, WY 83013; 307/543-2861 or 733-8761 or toll-free 1-800-443-2311.

HIKING

There are approximately 200 miles of hiking trails in Grand Teton National Park. For detailed information, visit Colter Bay and Moose Visitor Centers. For suggested reading, I recommend *Teton Trails* by Bryan Harry, former Asst. Chief Park Naturalist.

Self-Guided Trails

Menor's Ferry Trail: 0.5mi/0.8 km loop; trailhead: Chapel of the Transfiguration parking lot in Moose. Learn about the history of Jackson Hole and early crossings of the Snake River.

Cascade Canyon Trail: 7.7mi/12.3km; trailhead: boat dock west shore of Jenny Lake. This trail to Lake Solitude has booklets available at the east shore boat dock of Jenny Lake.

Cunningham Cabin Trail: 1.5mi/2.4km; trailhead: 6 mi. S of Moran Junction. Learn about the early ranching history of Jackson Hole.

Lunchtree Hill Trail: Short, paved loop; trailhead north of Jackson Lake Lodge via west patio. Learn how Jackson Hole got its name, etc.

Colter Bay Nature Trail: 1mi/1.6km; trailhead: .5 mi. W of Visitor Center. Learn about the natural history of the land and lakeshore. (Trail is on an isthmus of land in Jackson Lake).

BRIEF HISTORY

A history of Grand Teton National Park is a chronicle of the Jackson Hole area. The first humans followed the retreating Ice Age some 8000 years ago. The first American explorer was John Colter, who was a member of the Lewis & Clark Expedition. In the winter of 1807-8, he left the Expedition in Montana and explored south to Wyoming. The name "Jackson Hole" was bestowed by Bill Sublette, who named it for fellow trapper David Jackson. The word "Hole" was used by mountain men to describe high valleys surrounded by mountains.

The town of Jackson was laid out in 1897. Although there was sentiment to add the area to Yellowstone (est. 1872), there was strong local opposition against it. In 1926, John D. Rockefeller, Jr., became interested in protecting the area, and he purchased over 30,000 acres, which he eventually donated to the Park. This was added in 1950 to the original Park acreage established on February 26, 1929.

AUTHOR'S COMMENTS

Every national park has its "claim to fame", and in Grand Teton it's the scenery and abundance of wildlife. Even the absolute amateur photographer can take breathtaking pictures. Not that the scenery is the only attraction. Though undersized compared to Big Brother on the north (Yellowstone), it has boating, fishing, swimming, 200 miles of hiking trails, float trips, lake cruises, mountain climbing, guided horse trips, cross-country skiing, snowmobiling, and ice fishing, to name a few.

Great Basin

N A T I O N A L   P A R K,   N E V A D A

LOCATION:	East central Nevada
ACCESS:	5 mi. W of Baker, NV on NV 488; 70 mi. S of Ely, NV
SEASON:	All year
HOURS:	24 hours/day; contact NPS for Lehman Cave daily tour schedule
ENTRANCE FEE:	None
FOOD:	Near Park Headquarters (April-Oct.)
LODGING & GAS:	None in Park
NEAREST PROPANE:	Baker, NV
CAMPGROUNDS:	5 in Park (including 1 primitive without water); Lower Lehman Creek open all year
ADJACENT FACILITIES:	In Baker, NV: motels; restaurants; store; gas; see below for campgrounds
VISITOR CENTER:	At Park Headquarters area
MUSEUM:	Exhibits at Visitor Center
PICNICKING:	At Park Headquarters area
GIFT SHOP:	At Park Headquarters area (April-Oct.)
TOURS:	Through Lehman Cave daily (1½ hrs.)—nominal fees
ACTIVITIES:	Hiking; cross-country skiing; fishing; interpretive programs
CLIMATE:	High desert climate; possible extreme winter conditions
ELEVATION:	6,200 to 13,063 ft.
SIZE:	77,109 acres
PETS:	Must be on leash; not permitted in the cave, public buildings or in backcountry
FACILITIES FOR DISABLED:	Wheelchair access to Visitor Center and first Lehman Cave room
INFORMATION:	*Superintendent* *Great Basin National Park* *Baker, NV 89311* *702/234-7331*

CAMPGROUNDS

• The following 4 campgrounds have pit toilets with piped water nearby and fees of $4 per night.
• Opening and closing dates of all campgrounds are dependant on the weather, and all have a limit of stay of 14 days.

Lower Lehman Creek (elev. 7300′) is located approximately 2 mi. from Park Headquarters on Wheeler Peak Scenic Drive. It has 11 sites, is open all year, and can accommodate RV's up to 30 ft.

Upper Lehman Creek (elev. 7700′) is located 3 mi. from Park Headquarters on Wheeler Peak Scenic Drive. It has 24 sites and is open from early May to October.

Wheeler Peak (elev. 9950′) is located 12 mi. from Park Headquarters on Wheeler Peak Scenic Drive. It has 37 sites and is open early June through mid-September.

Baker Creek (elev. 7600′) is located 4 mi. from Park Headquarters on Baker Creek Road (graded gravel). It has 20 sites and is open mid-May through fall.

Primitive Campground:

Snake Creek (elev. 7700′) is located 1.5 mi. NW of Garrison, UT on UT 21, 1 mi. NW on NV 487, and 12 mi. SW on Snake Creek Road. The campground is open May-Oct. with no fee, no water and primitive facilities.

ADJACENT FACILITIES

Cave Lake SRA (State Park): 8 mi. S of Ely, NV on US 93, 6 mi. E on a gravel road; open all year; 20 sites; basic facilities; $4/night fee; write Panaca, NV 89042

Photo: Mark Richardson

GREAT BASIN

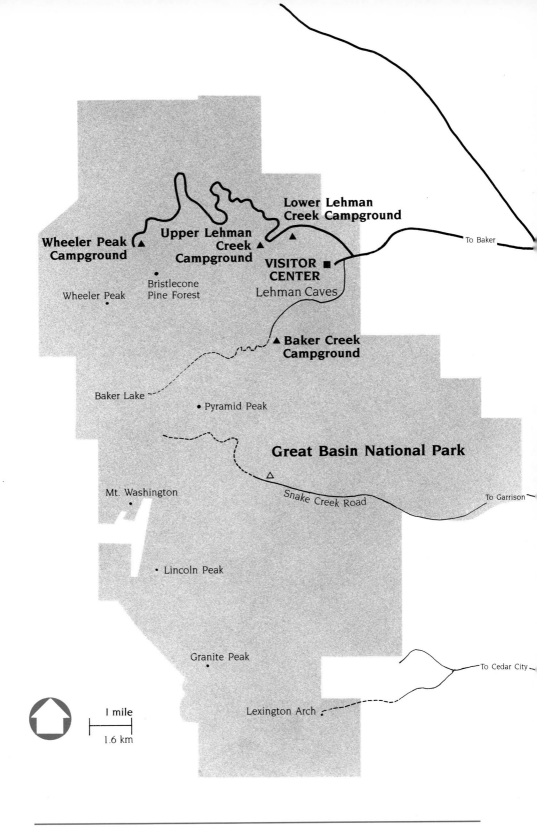

Wheeler Peak Campground

Upper Lehman Creek Campground

Lower Lehman Creek Campground

To Baker

VISITOR CENTER
Lehman Caves

Bristlecone Pine Forest

Wheeler Peak

▲ **Baker Creek Campground**

Baker Lake

• Pyramid Peak

Great Basin National Park

Mt. Washington

Snake Creek Road

To Garrison

• Lincoln Peak

Granite Peak

To Cedar City

Lexington Arch

1 mile

1.6 km

Great Basin National Park has approximately 65 miles of hiking trails. Unique hikes extend from the flank of Wheeler Peak past Alpine Lakes to a rare and ancient bristlecone pine forest or to the summit of Wheeler Peak (13,063 ft.).

Backcountry hiking and camping are permitted. Suggested reading is the Sierra Club tote book *Hiking the Great Basin*.

BRIEF HISTORY

There is evidence that prehistoric man occupied this area as early as thirty to forty thousand years ago. From approximately 8000 B.C. to 400 A.D., the Desert Culture inhabited the area. It was followed by the Fremont Culture, which lasted until approximately 1200 A.D. From approximately 1200 A.D. to the present, the Shoshone Indians have occupied the area.

Early explorers included the Escalante Dominguez expedition of 1776, which came within approximately 90 miles of the Park. In 1826-27 "Mountain Man" Jedediah Smith skirted the Snake Valley, and he was followed by the John C. Fremont party in 1840. The White Mountain Mission of the Church of Jesus Christ of Latter Day Saints entered the Snake Valley in 1855.

Absalom Lehman moved to the area sometime between 1866 and 1869, and he is credited with discovering the caves which bear his name. Wheeler Peak is named after Lt. George M. Wheeler, a surveyor for the U.S. Army, who spent from 1869-1879 mapping the area. The valley was settled by 1878.

Lehman Caves was declared a national monument on January 24, 1922 by President Warren G. Harding. The Wheeler Peak area was established as a scenic area on February 13, 1959, and both areas were encompassed in Great Basin National Park on October 27, 1986.

AUTHOR'S COMMENTS

Great Basin National Park was recently established and, as such, the information presented is very brief. It basically encompasses former Lehman Caves National Monument and Wheeler Peak Scenic Area. Naturally, as time goes on, more information will be made available by the National Park Service.

If you see cattle grazing in the Park, don't call a ranger. Unique to Great Basin National Park is that cattle grazing is allowed as a condition of the Park's creation.

One of my friends has spent many years exploring and hiking in the area. His work as a geologist has taken him extensively through Nevada, Utah, Arizona and New Mexico. He ranks this new national park area as one of the most interesting and beautiful places he has been. We hope you share his enthusiasm.

Haleakala

LOCATION: East Maui, Hawaiian Islands

ACCESS: Haleakala Crater from Kahului: 3 hrs. round trip via Hawaii 37, 377, and 378; Kipahulu District from central Maui: 60 mi. on Hawaii 36; Kipahulu District from Kihei, Lahaina, or Kaanapali: 85-90 mi. on Hawaii 36

SEASON: All year

HOURS: 24 hours/day

ENTRANCE FEES: $3/vehicle/day; $1/person all others/day; $10 annual; $25 Golden Eagle

GAS, FOOD & LODGING: None available in Park

CAMPGROUNDS: Primitive campgrounds and cabins year-round; no fees for campgrounds; 2-3 day limit of stay

ADJACENT FACILITIES & SERVICES: These can be reached by car in approximately 30 to 45 minutes. From Park Entrance (Haleakala Crater): restaurant & lodge, 12 miles on HI 377—Kula; gas station, 18 miles on HI 37—Pukalani. From Kipahulu (Oheo Gulch): restaurant, lodge & gas, 10 miles on HI 31—Hana

VISITOR CENTER: On rim: Crater District and House of the Sun; at Oheo: Kipahulu District

PICNICKING: Hosmer Grove; Park Headquarters (Crater District); Oheo Gulch (Kipahulu District)

TOURS: Crater District: at crater rim and Hosmer Grove; Kipahulu District: at trail side (summer only). Dependent on availability of staff

ACTIVITIES: Hiking; backpacking; horseback riding; swimming (Kipahulu District)

CLIMATE: Cool, often foggy at high elevations; average rainfall varies from 12 inches near Kapaloa to 300 inches at Paliku

ELEVATION: Sea level to 10,023 ft.

SIZE: 45 sq. miles

ANNUAL VISITATION: Approximately one and one-quarter million

PETS: Permitted on leash except in backcountry

FACILITIES FOR DISABLED: Restrooms; water fountains; paved walkways; parking stalls with ramps

INFORMATION: *Supt. Haleakala National Park*
Box 369
Makawao, HI 96768
808/572-9306; Kipahulu: 808/248-8260

Hosmer Grove is located ½ mile inside the north entrance on a paved road ½ mile east of the main Park road in a relatively flat, grassy area. It consists of five spots with a limit of 25 people, or a group limit of 15, and is open all year. Facilities include spots for tents, tables, grills, drinking water, chemical toilets, a cooking shelter with grill, and parking. No fee is required, and the campground is on a first-come basis. There is a three-day per month limit. From the main Park road it's the only campground to which you don't have to hike or horseback. The campground also serves as a trailhead to the Hosmer Grove nature trail.

Holua is located near Holua Cabin, which is approximately 4 miles from the Halemauu trailhead, just off the main Park road. The campground is limited to 25 people and is open all year. It is a primitive campground with pit toilets and drinking water. Campers must bring sleeping bags and tents. There is no campground fee, but a permit is required for use of the campground. There is a limit of 2 nights per location and 3 nights per month. There are no pets allowed and no open fires.

Kipahulu is located near Oheo Gulch in the south east portion of the Park off Highway 31. The campground consists of 50 sites and is open all year. It has pit toilets and no water. There is no campground fee. Camping is limited to 3 nights per month. Fishing and swimming are available.

Paliku is located near Paliku Cabin approximately 10 miles from both the Sliding Sands and Halemauu trailheads. It has the same facilities and rules as Holua Campground (see above).

CABINS

Three primitive crater cabins, Paliku, Kapalaoa and Holua, are maintained by the Park Service for visitor use on an advance reservation basis only. Each cabin is alloted to one party only with a limit of twelve people per night. Cabins are equipped with bunks, limited water, firewood, cookstove, eating and cooking utensils, and pit toilets. Rates (subject to change) are $5.00 per night for each adult and $2.50 for children 12 or under, with a nightly minimum of $15.00. A $15.00 key and cleaning deposit is required plus a $2.50 charge per person per night for firewood. Reservations are limited to 3 days per month with a limit of 2 consecutive days and are made *by mail only at least 90 days in advance*. Write Haleakala National Park, P.O. Box 369, Makawao, Maui, Hawaii 96768 for reservations or more detailed information.

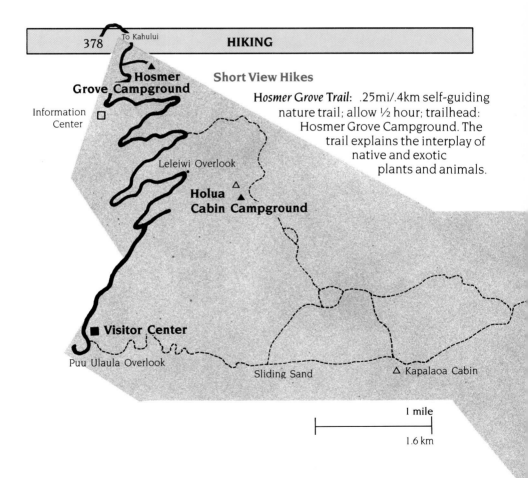

378   **HIKING**

Short View Hikes

Hosmer Grove Trail: .25mi/.4km self-guiding nature trail; allow ½ hour; trailhead: Hosmer Grove Campground. The trail explains the interplay of native and exotic plants and animals.

Halemauu Overlook Trail: 1mi/1.6km one way; allow 1.5 hours; easy; trailhead: at 8,000 ft. just off the Park road between Park Headquarters and Leleiwi Overlook. The hike is mostly level to the Overlook with its view of the colorful Crater.

White Hill Trail: .25mi/.4km one way; allow ½ hour minimum; easy; trailhead: Haleakala Visitor Center. Take your time on this trail, as you are just under 10,000 ft. above sea level.

Crater Hikes

There are Crater Rim hikes conducted by Park Rangers available during the summer months. They vary from .5mi/8.0km to 2.0mi/3.2km, and last from approximately one-half hour to two hours. Check at Park Headquarters for the schedule.

Sliding Sands Trail: Starts at the Visitor Center parking lot and descends into the Crater and returns. The hiker should take into consideration that the return is uphill at nearly 10,000 feet when judging the distance of this hike. There are excellent spots for picture-taking all along the way.

Halemauu Trail to Holua Cabin and Return: 8.0mi/13.0km round trip; allow 4-5 hours; trailhead: parking lot between Park Headquarters and Leleiwi Overlook on Park Road. The trail descends steeply to the Crater floor and Holua Cabin.

Halemauu Trail to Paliku Cabin: 10.2mi/16.3km one way; allow 5 hours going (7 for return); trailhead (see above). This hike is not recommended except as an overnight hike, and a permit is required. The trail descends steeply into the Crater and goes past Holua Cabin, Silversword Loop, Bottomless Pit, Honokahua and the Oili Puu Cinder Cone.

Sliding Sands Trail Return Halemauu Trail: 12.0mi/19.2km; 8 hours; recommended for good hikers only; trailhead: Visitor Center parking lot. It descends steeply into Haleakala Crater and exits on the Halemauu Trail.

Kaupo Trail: 8.0mi/12.8km; allow 4 hours; trailhead: Paliku Cabin. The trail descends through Kaupo Valley to the Park boundary and another 4.0mi/6.4km

Paliku Cabin Campground

Kaupo Gap

Haleakala National Park

Kipahula Valley

Waimoka Falls

Kipahulu Campground 31
To Hana

to the Coastal Highway. Only the first 3½ miles are maintained by the Park Service.

Kipahulu Area

There are ranger-guided hikes during the summer months. Check with the Kipahulu office or rangers for current schedules.

Waimoku Falls: 4.0mi/6.4km round trip; allow 2½ hours; trailhead: Oheo parking lot. It proceeds .5mi/.8km to Makahiku Falls Overlook and continues another 1.5mi/2.4km to Waimoku Falls.

Oheo Trail: 1.0mi/1.6km round trip; allow 45 minutes; trailhead: Lower Pools (and trail ends at the ocean). This hike is good for swimming and fishing.

PARK HISTORY

(See Hawaii Volcanoes National Park)

AUTHOR'S COMMENTS

The hardest thing to do in Haleakala National Park is to hike the 19 sq. miles of the Haleakala Crater on its 32 miles of trails. The second hardest thing to do is pronounce the name correctly. The word in Hawaiian means "House of the Sun" Legend has it that demigod Maui lassoed the sun's rays from the sunlight of Haleakala. He would not release the sun until it promised to cross the sky more slowly. Maui left some of the ropes attached to remind the sun of its promise. These can be seen just before the sun sets trailing into the Pacific.

Hawaii Volcanoes

LOCATION:	Southeastern Hawaii
ACCESS:	From Hilo (30 mi.) and Kona (100 mi.) on Highway 11
SEASON:	All year
HOURS:	24 hours/day
ENTRANCE FEES:	$5/vehicle/week; $2/person all others/week; $15 annual; $25 Golden Eagle
FOOD & GAS:	Volcano Village, located 1 mi. north of the Park on Highway 11; Volcano House; stores at Kalapana, 4 mi. east of the coastal section of the Park.
LODGING:	THE VOLCANO HOUSE: located on rim of Kilauea caldera; open all year and usually full; reservations advised: The Volcano House, Hawaii National Park,HI 96718, 808/967-7174
CAMPGROUNDS:	Limited sites and cabins; no fee; open year round
ADJACENT FACILITIES:	In Volcano , 1 mi. north of park on Hawaii 11: groceries, gas and camping supplies; in Kalapana, 4 mi. east of coastal section of park: groceries and meals
VISITOR CENTERS:	Wahaula at coastal Park entrance; Kilauea on north rim of caldera; Thomas A. Jaggar on west rim of caldera, 3 mi. W of Kilauea Visitor Center
MUSEUM:	In Kilauea Visitor Center; cultural exhibits in Waha'ula Visitor Center; geology/volcanology exhibits in Thomas A. Jaggar Museum
PICNICKING:	Sites available throughout Park
TOURS:	Conducted by tour companies (some in Japanese)
ACTIVITIES:	Hiking; backpacking; interpretive programs
CLIMATE:	Semitropical to alpine
ELEVATION:	Sea level to 13,677 ft. (Mauna Loa)
SIZE:	344 sq. miles
ANNUAL VISITATION:	Near one and one-third million
PETS:	Permitted on leash; not permitted in backcountry
FACILITIES FOR DISABLED:	Campgrounds, visitor centers, restrooms, overlooks
INFORMATION:	*Supt. Hawaii Volcanoes National Park*, HI 96718; 808/967-7311

CAMPGROUNDS

NOTE: Dead and down firewood may be gathered, but little is available around campgrounds and picnic areas. It is advisable to bring contained fire stoves (gas, propane, etc.) for cooking purposes.

Kamoamoa is located 26 mi. SE of Park Headquarters off of Chain of Craters Road in a shady area. It has 10 spaces and is open all year. It provides picnic tables, grills, flush toilets and water. There is no fee and camping is on a first-come basis with a limit of stay of 7 days per year. The campground is accessible for handicapped.

Kipuka Nene is located 12 miles south of Park Service Headquarters on the Hilina Road 5 miles from its junction with Chain of Craters Road. It has 6 open tent sites and is open all year. Facilities include a shelter area with fireplace and tables, several tables and grills outside shelter area, pit toilets, and water from a water tank. There is no fee and camping is on a first-come basis with a limit of stay of 7 days per year. The campground serves as a trailhead for the trail to Halape.

Namakani Paio is located 3 miles west of Park Service Headquarters on Hawaii 11 in a level, shady area. It has 10 individual sites, 2 group sites, and is open all year. Facilities include a covered shelter with fireplace and tables, a table and grill at each site, flush toilets and water. There is no fee. Camping is limited to 7 days per year, and the campground is accessible for handicapped.

Ten camper cabins, which are rented by The Volcano House, are adjacent to the campground, with grills and tables provided for each cabin. There is a comfort station with flush toilets and showers serving the registered guests of the cabins only. There is a public telephone available.

Directly across from the campground entrance is the trailhead to Volcano Observatory and Crater Rim Trail, both .5 mile.

HIKING

Kilauea Summit Trails

Crater Rim Loop Trail: 11.6mi/18.6km; 8 hours; strenuous; ascent 500 ft.; trailhead: in front of Volcano House. This is the best trail for acquainting oneself with the Kilauea crater. Proceeding counter clockwise is recommended in order to cross the Kau Desert in the cool of the morning.

Thurston Lava Tube Trail: .3mi/.48km; 15 minutes; easy; trailhead: in the parking lot off Crater Rim Dr. 1.8 mi. from Park Headquarters. This is a hike through a lush fern forest leading to a 450-foot lava tube. (It's a good hike for observing birds if taken in the early morning or late afternoon.) If you were only going to take one short hike, this should be the one.

Devastation Trail: .6mi/1.0km one way; 20 min; easy; trailhead: Pu'u Pua'i Overlook parking area 3.1 miles from Park Headquarters on Crater Rim Dr. or Devastation Trail parking area. This unique hike leads through a devastation area caused by the 1959 Kilauea Iki eruption. It's a boardwalk trail that is suitable for strollers or wheelchairs with experienced assistance. You can start at either end and have your driving companion continue driving and pick you up at the other.

Halema'uma'u Trail: 3.2mi/5.1km one way; 2 hours; moderate difficulty; trailhead: west of Volcano House. This is a self-guiding trail across the floor of the Kilauea caldera ending at the Halema'uma'u parking lot. It's a hot and dry trail, so take water. The trail crosses lava flows from 1885, 1919, 1954, 1971, 1974, 1975 and 1982.

Byron Ledge Trail: 2.5mi/4.0km one way; 1½ hours; strenuous; trailhead: begins and ends on Halema'uma'u Trail. This is basically a connecting trail running along Byron Ledge, which separates Kilauea from Kilauea Iki.

Kilauea Iki Trail: 5.0mi/8.0km round trip; 2-3 hours; strenuous; trailhead: Thurston Lava Tube (may also start at Visitor Center for a 5.0mi/8.0km hike). The trail descends 400 ft. through native forest with good bird activity onto a solid kind of lava crust where you walk a mile and a half across next to the Pu'u Pua i vent site of the 1959 eruption. The trail then ascends the other side for about 300 feet.

Mauna Iki Trail: (*Footprint* Trail): 3.6mi/5.8km round trip; 2 hours; easy; trailhead: on Hawaii 11, 9.1 miles southwest of Park Headquarters, ending at the top of Mauna Iki (1.6mi/2.6km round trip to the Footprints). The trail leads to footprints preserved in ash of a Hawaiian war party caught and killed in the ash eruption of 1790 in the Kau Desert. The trail continues to the top of Mauna Iki (3032 ft.).

Mauna Loa Strip Road Trails

Bird Park Trail: 1.1mi/1.8km loop; 1 hour; easy; trailhead: on Mauna Loa Strip Road. This is a self-guiding nature trail transcending through a rich concentration of flora. Many varieties of birds may be heard although few are seen as they remain in the tall forest crown of the Kepuka.

Mauna Loa Trail: 18.3mi/29.28km one way; 3–4 days; very strenuous; trailhead: the end of the Mauna Loa Strip Road at 6662 ft., ending near the summit at 13,250 ft. The first day's hike should reach Red Hill with an ascent of 3370 feet. (7 miles at 10,035' elev.). The second day's climb to the summit is another 11 miles ascending 3645 feet higher. Overnight hikers must register at Kilauea Visitor Center.

Kalapana Area

Ke Ala Kahiko Trail: 1.3mi/2.1km loop; 1 hour; easy; trailhead: behind the Waha'ula Visitor Center. The trail passes near templegrounds and continues to the shoreline through Poupou-Kauka Village.

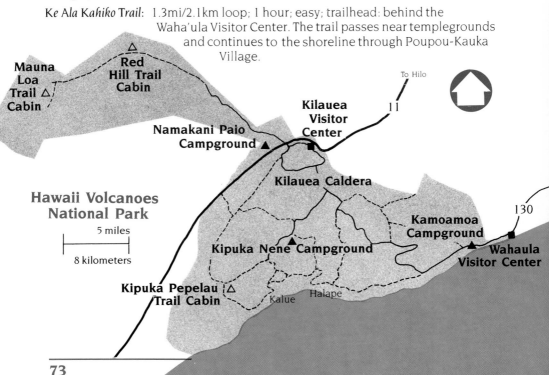

Pu'uloa Petroglyphs Trail: .5mi/.8km one way; 1 hour; moderate; trailhead (road sign): 8.5 miles west of Waha'ula Visitor Center. The petroglyphs are on mounds of varying sizes and shapes chipped in lava.

Chain of Craters Road

Favorite Hike of a Park Ranger:

"**Pu'u Huluhulu Cinder Cone:** 1.2 miles one way; allow 2-3 hours; easy; ascent 150 feet plus; trailhead: from the Mauna Ulu parking lot. Pu'u Huluhulu is a prehistoric cinder and spatter cone 150 feet higher than the surrounding area. On a clear day, from the top you have views out to the Pacific Ocean as well as of Mauna Loa and Mauna Kea. There are also views of Pu'u O'o, the new cone built up since 1983, and you can look all the way down to Cape Kumukahi on the eastern tip of the island. It's a nice kind of pack-your-lunch trail, and you can explore the 73-74 lava flows."

Note: Mauna Kea is the tallest volcanic mountain and Mauna Kea and Mauna Loa are the largest (in terms of volume) volcanic mountains on earth.

BRIEF HISTORY

The first inhabitants of the Hawaiian Islands were Polynesians, who sailed 2400 miles from the Marquesas Islands, probably around A.D. 750. Around A.D. 1200 another group arrived from Tahiti and were the dominant people. James Cook arrived in 1778 and things were never the same, as new animals, plants, religions, customs, and diseases spread rapidly in an almost completely isolated environment.

Photo: Hawaii Natural History Association

Volcanic eruptions on the island were first documented by missionaries William Ellis and Asa Thurston in 1823, and Halemaumau remained a continuously boiling lava lake. In 1912 the Hawaiian Volcano Observatory was established. Political forces and professional input toward the establishment of the area as a national park began to accelerate, and the focus of national attention on all volcanic regions increased when Mt. Lassen erupted in 1916. Hawaii Volcanoes National Park and Lassen Volcanic National Park were both established that year.

The original Park boundaries have been extended over the years to their present locations. In 1961 Haleakala on Maui was separated from Hawaii Volcanoes National Park and established as a separate national park.

AUTHOR'S COMMENTS

What time is the next eruption? That's the question asked the Park Ranger by the visitor next to me. Though eruptions can be forecast to some extent, their exact time is still a matter of chance. Naturally a visit to the Park is certainly a more interesting one during an eruption, but it is still worth seeing at any time.

When's the best time to see the Park?

Whenever you can get to Hawaii.

"NATIONAL PARKS"
by John Muir

The park is the poor man's refuge
Here we are all together blind and deaf
To the sweet looks and voices of nature
The sun shines not on us
But in us
The river flows not past
But through us
The trees wave and the flowers bloom
In our bodies as well as in our souls
And every bird's song
Or wind's song
And tremendous storm song
Of the rocks in the heart of the mountains
Is our song
The song of God
Sounding out forever
The fine place for feasting
If only one be poor enough.

(This poem is found in the Volcano Art Center located near the Kilauea Visitor Center in historic Volcano House (1877).

Kings Canyon

N A T I O N A L   P A R K ,   C A L I F

LOCATION:	East central California
ACCESS:	California 180 from Fresno (55 miles); Generals Highway via Sequoia National Park
SEASON:	Grant Grove all year; Cedar Grove May to October
HOURS:	24 hours/day
ENTRANCE FEES:	$5/vehicle/week; $2/person all others/week; $15 annual; $25 Golden Eagle
GAS, FOOD & LODGING:	Grant Grove Village, Cedar Grove Village and Stony Creek
NEAREST PROPANE:	Grant Grove Village
CAMPGROUNDS:	7 campgrounds in Grant Grove and Cedar Grove areas; no hook-ups; some primitive camping; wilderness campground
ADJACENT FACILITIES:	Several U.S.F.S. campgrounds (see below)
VISITOR CENTERS:	Grant Grove Visitor Center; Cedar Grove Ranger Station
PICNICKING:	Columbine; Big Stump; Sunset; Roads End in Cedar Grove
GIFT SHOPS:	In Grant Grove Village and Cedar Grove Village
TOURS:	Daily from Giant Forest, Stony Creek or Grant Grove Lodge to Grant Grove and Cedar Grove areas including Kings River Canyon areas; ranger-led activities
ACTIVITIES:	Hiking; fishing (license required); horseback riding; mountain climbing; cross-country skiing; interpretive programs
WILDERNESS CAMPING:	Permits are required for overnight trips into the backcountry, and reservations for a pre-arranged trail entry date must be made by mail only.
CLIMATE:	Hot summers with cool nights; snowy winters
ELEVATION:	4,600 ft. to 14,242 ft.
SIZE:	717 sq. miles
ANNUAL VISITATION:	Near one million
PETS:	Must be on leash; not allowed on trails or public buildings
FACILITIES FOR DISABLED:	Most buildings; marked campsites
INFORMATION:	*Supt. Sequoia/Kings Canyon National Parks* *Three Rivers, CA 93271* *209/565-3341* *Park Emergency: 911*

• All campgrounds are on a first-come basis and usually fill weekends and holidays during the summer.
• The fee is $6 at all campgrounds.
• There is a camping limit of 14 days in summer; 30 days the remainder of the year.
• All campsites have tables and fireplaces; all campgrounds furnish flush toilets and piped water.
• There are no hook-ups in the Park.
• Pay showers are available in Grant Grove Village and Cedar Grove Village.
• Wood-gathering is permitted outside of sequoia groves; firewood is for sale in markets.

Grant Grove Area (elev. 6500') is open all year. Facilities and services in Grant Grove Village include stores, gas station, restaurants, gift shop, post office and visitor center.

Azalea is located ¼ mi. northwest of Grant Grove Village in a level area of large pine and cedar. It has 113 sites and is the only campground in the Park open all year. The campground has a dump station. Some campsites have handicapped access.

Crystal Springs is located ½ mi. north of Grant Grove Village in a pine and cedar forested area. It has 63 sites and is open mid-June to mid-September.

Sunset is located ¼ mi. south of Grant Grove Village in a level pine and cedar forest. It has 192 sites and is open mid-May to mid-October. The campground has an amphitheater serving all the area campgrounds with evening campfire programs.

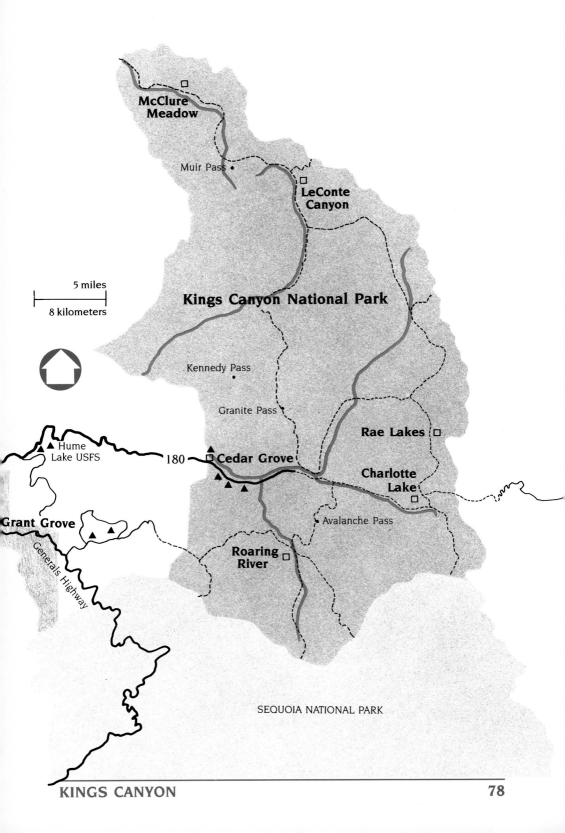

5 miles

8 kilometers

McClure
Meadow

Muir Pass •

LeConte
Canyon

Kings Canyon National Park

Kennedy Pass
•

Granite Pass

Rae Lakes □

Hume
Lake USFS

180 □ Cedar Grove

Charlotte
Lake □

Grant Grove

Avalanche Pass •

Generals Highway

Roaring
River □

SEQUOIA NATIONAL PARK

Cedar Grove Area (elev. 4631') is open May to November, depending on weather conditions and spring snowpack. Facilities and services in Cedar Grove Village include market/gift shop, gas station, snack bar, laundromat and ranger station.

Canyon View is located on Hwy. 180 ½ mi. east of Village Road junction in a level, wooded area. It has 37 sites and is open mid-May to mid-September. Group campsites are available for groups of 20 or more and reservations are required (Canyon View Campground, Group Sites, Cedar Grove Ranger Station, Box 948, Kings Canyon National Park, CA 93633).

Moraine is located 1 mi. east of Village Road junction in an area gently sloping towards the Kings River. It has 120 sites and is open mid-May to mid-September.

Sentinel is located ¼ mi. west of Cedar Grove Village, adjacent to the Ranger Station, in a wooded area. It has 83 sites and is open mid-May to mid-September. The campground has an amphitheater serving all campgrounds in the area with evening campfire programs. Some campsites have handicapped access.

Sheep Creek is located along Hwy. 180 one mile west of Cedar Grove Village in a fairly level, forested area. It has 111 sites and is open May to November depending on use and weather. The campground has a dump station.

ACCOMMODATIONS

Grant Grove Lodge: In Grant Grove Village; open year round (closed Mon. & Tues. in winter); rustic cabins with bath and housekeeping cabins; commercial showers available 12 p.m. to 3:30 p.m. April–October (no restriction remainder of year)

Cedar Grove Lodge: In Cedar Grove Village; open mid-May to Oct.; motel-type accommodations.

Stony Creek Lodge and Campground: In Sequoia National Forest midway between Sequoia and Kings Canyon National Parks; open mid-May to Oct.; motel-type accommodations, restaurant, market/gift shop, gas station
   Reservations for above: Guest Services, Sequoia National Park, CA 93262; 209/561-3314

Kings Canyon Lodge: On Hwy. 180 between Grant Grove and Cedar Grove; closed in winter; rustic housekeeping cottages, cafe, service station; reservations: 209/335-2404

Wilsonia Lodge: ½ mi. from Grant Grove Village via. Hwy. 180 and Wilsonia Rd.; motel-type accommodations; open all year; reservations: Wilsonia Lodge, Kings Canyon National Park, CA 93633, 209/335-2310

ADJACENT FACILITIES

U.S. Forest Service Campgrounds
Stony Creek: Off Generals Hwy. approximately half way between Grant Grove and Lodgepole in Sequoia National Forest; 79 tent sites, 70 trailer sites, and group camping sites on 13 acres (Reservations required for groups: 209/561-3314):

open 5/15–10/15; $6 fee; 14-day limit of stay; tables, water and pit toilets.

Hume Lake: Off Hwy. 180 between Grant Grove and Cedar Grove; 74 tent sites and 29 trailer sites on 30 acres; open 5/15 to Labor Day; $5 fee; 14-day limit of stay; tables and flush toilets.

Princess: 5.5 mi. NW of Hume Lake on FR 13501, 1 mi. W on Hwy. 180; 90 tent sites and 111 trailer sites; open 5/25–9/3; dump station; store, cafe & ice within 5 miles.

Big Meadow: 1.4 mi. S of Grant Grove on Hwy. 180, 6.5 mi. SE on USFH78 4.4 mi. NE on FR 14501; 25 tent sites and 25 trailer sites; open mid-May to Oct.

HIKING

Grant Grove Area

Manzanita Trail: 3.3mi/5.3km round trip; 2 hours; moderate; ascent 800'; trailhead: far end of Visitor Center parking lot. This trail begins in forest, with some steep areas, and then gently traverses Manzanita Hill to the top of Park Ridge. Return may be via the Azalea Trail.

Park Ridge Trail: 4.7mi/7.5km round trip; 3 hours; easy; ascent 200'; trailhead: Panoramic Point parking area. This trail affords excellent vistas with interpretive displays giving an overall perspective of Kings Canyon National Park. The trail continues along the ridge to the fire lookout, and return may be via the dirt fire road.

Dead Giant Loop Trail: 2.2mi/3.5km round trip; 1.5 hours; easy; descent 400'; trailhead: extreme end of Grant Tree parking lot. This trail descends to the Dead Giant, an unusually large sequoia killed by man, proceeds to Sequoia Lake Overlook, and returns via another ridge trail with views of lower Kings Canyon.

Sunset Trail: 6.0mi/9.6km round trip; 3-4 hours; fairly strenuous; descent 1400'; trailhead: across main highway from Visitor Center. This trail affords an environment of forest, wildflowers, waterfalls (spectacular in spring and early summer) and sculptured rock pools. Return may be via this trail or the old road to General Grant Tree parking area.

General Grant Tree Trail: 2.3mi/3.7km round trip; 1.5 hours; easy; descent 300'; trailhead: Visitor Center or Grant Tree parking area. This trail passes Columbine Picnic area along a small stream and descends to the grove of giant sequoias, joining the self-guiding loop trail around the General Grant Tree near the parking area.

North Grove Loop: 1.5mi/2.4km round trip; 1–1.5 hours; easy; descent 400'; trailhead: extreme end of lower Grant Tree parking area. This trail follows a one-way road through giant sequoias and a mixed forest and intersects an old fire road leading to the site of an 1890's mill town. Return may be via the road to the Dead Giant Loop Trail.

Big Stump Trail: 1.0mi/1.6km round trip; 1 hour; easy; trailhead: Big Stump Parking Lot. This numbered interpretive trail displays the results of the intensive logging operations of the 1880's and gives visual emphasis to one of the main reasons for creating Kings Canyon and Sequoia National Parks.

Cedar Grove Area

Zumwalt Meadow Trail: 1.5mi/2.4km round trip; 1–2 hours; easy; trailhead: Zumwalt Meadow parking lot. This numbered interpretive loop trail gives evidence of glacier action and erosion as well as an insight into the Native Americans of the region.

River Trail: 1.0mi/1.6km (.5 hour) round trip to Roaring River Falls; 3.2mi/5.1km (2–3 hours) round trip to Zumwalt Meadow; easy; trailhead: Roaring River Falls parking area. This trail offers views of the impressive falls and the interest of a varied forest.

Hotel Creek Trail: 5.5mi/8.8km one way; 4–6 hours; ascent 1200'; trailhead: .25 mi. down canyon from pack station. This trail passes through an experimental forest restoration area on the way to the cascade (80 ft. ascent) and then begins a series of switchbacks to the top wall of the canyon for the valley view.

Mist Falls Trail: 8.0mi/12.8km round trip; 4 hours; ascent 600'; trailhead: Road's End. This very pleasant trail follows the South Fork of the Kings River to Mist Falls. The hiker may then continue another 3 miles to Paradise Valley (total ascent 1500 ft.). intersecting the John Muir Trail.

Redwood Canyon Trail: 10.0mi/16.0km loop; 5 hours; trailhead: Redwood Saddle. Highlights of this trail include the Sugar Bowl Grove (almost a pure stand of sequoias) and Redwood Canyon itself, which contains one of the most beautiful of all the giant sequoia groves.

BRIEF HISTORY

Native Americans have occupied the Sierra Nevada mountains for use as summer camps for thousands of years. They came to escape the valley heat, as do tourists of today, and to take advantage of the food resources the retreating winter snows provided. There were four main tribes, the Monache, Tubatu Labac, Paiutes and Yokuts, and they traded and visited with each other.

Early Spanish explorers did little to explore the region, but an expedition led by Gabrial Moraga in 1806 named the Kings River "El Rio de Los Santos Reyes", the river of the Holy Kings. Expeditions led by Jedediah Smith in 1827 and John C. Fremont in 1844 did little to penetrate the high country.

In 1864 an expedition of the California State Geological Survey headed by William Brewer issued a detailed report which discovered and named, among others, Mt. Whitney (14,495 ft.). John Muir was also an early explorer making extensive trips in 1873 and 1875. Excessive lumbering and sheep grazing of the area during the 1870's and '80's provoked conservationists led by John Muir and George Stewart of Visalia into efforts to create a national park. Their endeavors were instrumental in 1890 in creating Sequoia National Park and General Grant National Park (which is now Grant Grove).

Early administration was by the war department who used troops to prevent illegal grazing and lumbering operations. However, administration as we know it today was spotty. In 1940 Kings Canyon National Park was established. Included within its boundaries were General Grant Grove and adjoining groves in Redwood Canyon. It was further expanded in 1965 to include Cedar Grove and Tephipite Valley.

AUTHOR'S COMMENTS

(See Sequoia National Park.)

Lassen Volcanic

LOCATION:	Northeastern California
ACCESS:	CA 89 from north and south; CA 36 and 44 from east and west
SEASON:	All year; only Southwest Entrance open in winter to ski area
HOURS:	24 hours/day
ENTRANCE FEES:	$5/vehicle/week; $2/person all others/week; $15 annual (summer only); $25 Golden Eagle; $1/vehicle winter use
FOOD:	Lassen Chalet (Southwest Entrance); Drakesbad Guest Ranch (reservations required); Manzanita Lake Camper Service Store
GAS:	Mazanita Lake Camper Service Store
NEAREST PROPANE:	Manzanita Lake Camper Service Store; Mineral Chevron
LODGING:	DRAKESBAD GUEST RANCH: 47 mi. from Southwest Entrance (18 mi. from Chester) in Warner Valley area; open late June to mid-Sept.; family-style dining room; heated pool; horseback riding; info/reservations: California Guest Services, Inc., Adobe Plaza, 2150 Main St., Red Bluff, CA 96080, 916/529-1512
CAMPGROUNDS:	8 in the Park; first-come basis; group camping (reservations required); open approximately June to October, depending on weather; no hook-ups
ADJACENT FACILITIES:	See below
VISITOR CENTERS:	Small, temporary structures at Southwest Entrance and Manzanita Lake Entrance (open summers only)
PICNICKING:	Five sites along the main Park road
GIFT SHOPS:	Lassen Chalet; Manzanita Lake Camper Service Store
TOURS:	Naturalist-led walks and hikes
ACTIVITIES:	Hiking; boating; lake and stream trout fishing; horseback riding; interpretative programs; backpacking (permit required); cross-country and alpine skiing
CLIMATE:	Pleasant in summer; heavy snow in winter
ELEVATION:	4,800 to 10,457 ft.
SIZE:	166 sq. miles
ANNUAL VISITATION:	Nearly one-half million
PETS:	Must be on leash; not allowed on trails or in public buildings
FACILITIES FOR DISABLED:	Information centers; restrooms; campgrounds; Drakesbad Ranch facilities; trail, programs and amphitheater with assistance

INFORMATION: *Supt. Lassen Volcanic National Park*
Mineral, CA 96063
916/595-4444
Park Emergency: 911 *or Park* HQ (8:00-4:30) 595-4444
Manzanita Lk. Rang. Sta. (8:00-4:30) 335-7373

• All campgrounds are on a first-come basis.
• There are no hook-ups in the Park.
• Most campsites have tables and fireplaces.
• Camping is limited to 14 days except at Lost Creek and Summit Lake, where the limit is 7 days.
• Dead and down firewood may be gathered, except manzanita wood.
• Group campsites can accommodate 25 people and the fee is $20/night, except Juniper Lake, which has no fee. Group camping is limited to tents only and reservations are required: Supt. Lassen Volcanic National Park, Box 100, Mineral, CA 96063-0100.

Butte Lake (elev. 6100′) is located in the NE corner of the Park. It has 98 individual sites, 2 group sites, and is open June to mid-October. The campground has flush toilets and piped water until September, then no water and pit toilets. The fee is $6 per night. Fishing, swimming, hiking and boating without motors are available.

Warner Valley (elev. 5650′) is located via partially-paved road 17 mi. from Chester. It has 15 sites and is open mid-June to October. The campground is not recommended for trailers. Facilities include piped water and pit toilets, and the fee is $4 per night. Stream fishing and hiking are available as well as meals (on reservation),cold drinks,telephone and horseback riding at Drakesbad Guest Ranch.

Juniper Lake (elev. 5700′) is located via dirt road 13 mi. north from Chester. It has 18 individual sites, one group site, and is open late-June to October. The campground is not recommended for trailers. It has pit toilets, and water obtained from the lake should be boiled. There is no fee. Fishing, swimming and boating without motors are available.

Manzanita Lake (elev. 5890′) is located adjacent to and S of Manzanita Lake at the NW Entrance to the Park. It has 179 sites and is open June to mid-October. Facilities include flush toilets and piped water, the fee is $6 per night, and the campground will accommodate trailers to 35 ft. Additional facilities include a dump station, showers, electric razor outlets, concession services, and naturalist programs. Boating without motors is available.

Crags Campground (elev. 5700′) is located 5 mi. from Manzanita Lake and is an *overflow campground* (open only when Manzanita Lake Campground is full). It has 45 sites and is open June to mid-October. Facilities include chemical toilets and piped water until September, then pit toilets and no water. The fee is $4 per night. The campground will accommodate trailers to 35 ft.

Lost Creek (elev. 5700′) is located 5 mi. from Manzanita Lake. It has 7 group sites only and is open mid-May to October. It has chemical toilets and piped water until September, then pit toilets and no water. The fee is $20 per group per night.

Southwest (elev. 6700′) is located at the SW Entrance. It has 21 sites and is open mid-June to October. This is a walk-in campground with flush toilets and piped water. The fee is $4 per night. Nearby Lassen Chalet has food service and a gift shop.

Summit Lake (elev. 6695′) is located 12 mi. S of Manzanita Lake. It has 94 sites and is open June to mid-September. The north end has flush toilets and piped water until September, then pit toilets and no water. The fee is $6 per night. The south end has chemical toilets and piped water until September, then pit toilets and no water. The fee is $4 per night. Swimming, hiking and naturalist programs are available.

South of Park

Lassen Mineral Lodge: 9 mi. W of SW Entrance on CA 36; motel; store; gas station with propane; restaurant & bar (open daily Memorial Day weekend through Oct.); pool; gift shop; post office; reservations: P.O. Box 160, Mineral, CA 96063; 916/595-4422.

McGoverns Vacation Chalets: 9 mi. W of SW Entrance on CA 36 (Mineral); see above for facilities in Mineral; reservations: 563 McClay Rd., Novato, CA 94947; 916/595-4497 or 415/897-8377.

Volcano Country Camping: 9 mi. W of SW Entrance on CA 36 (Mineral); open 5/25-10/1; full hook-ups; showers; laundromat; ice; firewood; see above for facilities in Mineral; reservations: P.O. Box 55, Mineral, CA 96063; 916/595-3347.

Childs Meadow Resort: 9 mi. E of SW Entrance on CA 36; limited operation in winter; motel & cabins; RV hook-ups; limited food service; showers; laundromat; pool; tennis; reservations: Rt. 5, Box 3000, Mill Creek, CA 96061; 916/595-4411.

Mill Creek Resort: 11 mi. E of SW Entrance on Hwy. 172 off 36; limited operation in winter; cabins; RV hook-ups; showers; store; gas; laundromat; coffee shop; post office; reservations: Mill Creek, CA 96061, 916/595-4449.

Lassen Lodge Cabins: 13 mi. W of SW Entrance on CA 36; reservations: Rt. 5, Box 65, Paynes Creek, CA 96075; 916/597-2944.

Canyon View Lodge: 17 mi. W of SW Entrance on Canyon View Loop off CA 36; restaurant (closed Mondays except holidays); Basque style family dinners; bar; reservations: Rt. 5, Box 28, Paynes Creek, CA 96075; 916/597-2400.

Fire Mountain Lodge: 15 mi. E of SW Entrance on CA 36; limited operation in winter; motel & cabins; trailer park; store; gas; restaurant; bar; reservations: Mill Creek, CA 96061; 916/258-2938.

Deer Creek Lodge: 19 mi. E of SW Entrance on CA 36; cabins; restaurant (open Thurs. through Mon. during summer months); gas; reservations: Mill Creek, CA 96061; 916/258-2939.

Black Forest Lodge: 20 mi. E of SW Entrance on CA 36; motel (open year-round); restaurant and bar (open daily from Memorial Day weekend, except Mon.); German food; reservations: Rt. 5, Box 5000, Mill Creek, CA 96061; 916/258-2941.

St. Bernard Lodge: 20 mi. E of SW Entrance on CA 36; hotel; camping; restaurant & bar (closed Tues.-Wed.); reservations: Rt. 5, Box 5500, Mill Creek, CA 96061; 916/258-3382.

Forest Service Campgrounds.

Battle Creek: 2 mi. W of Mineral on CA 36; open 5/25-10/1; 50 tent, 38 trailer sites; 5 mi. to store, cafe, laundry, ice.

Mill Creek: .5 mi. E of Mill Creek on Hwy. 172; open 5/25-10/1; 12 tent, 12 trailer sites; 1 mi. to store, cafe, ice.

Gurnsey Creek: 14 mi. W of Chester on CA 36; open 5/25-10/1; 52 tent, 25 trailer sites; 1 mi. to store, cafe, ice.

North of Park

Hat Creek Resort: 13 mi. N of Manzanita Lake on CA 44; motel; cabins; trailer park; reservations: P.O. Box 15, Old Station, CA 96071; 916/335-2359.

Mt. Lassen KOA: 14 mi. W of Manzanita Lake on CA 44; open all year; hook-ups; showers; propane; groceries; reservations: Rt. 1, Box 400, Shingletown, CA 96088; 916/474-3133.

Rim Rock Ranch: 14 mi. N of Manzanita Lake on CA 44; cabins; groceries; fishing; supplies; food service across the road; reservations: Rt. 2, Box 200, Old Station, CA 96071; 916/335-2349.

Mill Creek Trailer Park: 15 mi. W of Manzanita Lake on Mill Creek Rd. off CA 44; open year-round; cabins; hook-ups; showers; laundromat; fishing; reservations: P.O. Box 565, Shingletown, CA 96088; 916/474-5384.

Shingletown: 17 mi. W of Manzanita Lake on CA 44; groceries; gas; restaurants; health clinic.

Old Honn Homestead: 28 mi. N of Manzanita Lake on Hwy. 89; motel; cabins; no food service; reservations: Hat Creek, CA 96040; 916/335-4277.

There are numerous *Forest Service campgrounds* on Hwy. 89 north of the Park, primarily along Hat Creek. All are open May-Oct. Honn is open year-round.

HIKING

There are approximately 150 miles of hiking trails in Lassen Volcanic National Park. Lassen is, for the most part, a day-hike Park.

However, by combining several day hikes, excellent overnight backpacking is afforded. The majority of the hiking trails are located in the uncrowded eastern part of the Park out of Drakesbad (Warner Valley), Juniper Lake and Butte Lake.

For detailed information, two books are available: *Hiking Trails of Lassen Volcanic National Park* by the author and *Lassen's Trails* by Stephen H. Matteson. Listed below are brief descriptions of the more popular trails.

Off the main Park road

Brokeoff: 3.5mi/5.7km one way; allow 3-4 hours; strenuous; 2800 ′ ascent; trailhead: Road Guide Marker #2, .5 mi. from southern boundary. This is considered by the author to be one of the best hikes in the Park. It combines almost all the features one would expect in a good mountain hike. It climbs a peak with views in every direction, crosses and follows springs running through meadows abundant with wildflowers, and passes unusual rock formations.

Sulphur Works: .2mi/.3km round trip; allow 20 min.; easy; trailhead: Road Guide Marker #5. This nature trail is a hydrothermal area with bubbling mud pots, fumaroles and hydrogen sulphide gas.

Bumpass Hell: 3.0mi/4.8km round trip; allow 2.5-3 hrs.; easy; 250′ ascent, then 200′ descent; trailhead: Road Guide Markers #'s 16 & 17. This self-guiding nature trail is one of Lassen's most popular hikes. Bumpass Hell is a hydrothermal area similar to the Sulphur Works but much larger.

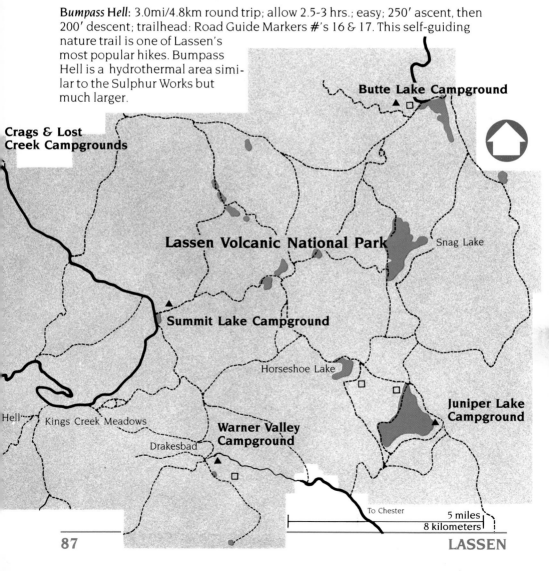

Butte Lake Campground

Crags & Lost Creek Campgrounds

Lassen Volcanic National Park

Snag Lake

Summit Lake Campground

Horseshoe Lake

Juniper Lake Campground

Hell

Kings Creek Meadows

Drakesbad

Warner Valley Campground

To Chester

5 miles
8 kilometers

LASSEN

Lassen Peak: 2.5mi/4.0km one way; allow 3-4 hours; strenuous; 1957' ascent; trailhead: Road Guide Marker #22. For many visitors, a visit to Lassen Peak is not complete without hiking Lassen Peak. Although the trail is somewhat tiresome trudging through cinders, the views at the summit make it worthwhile.

Terrace, Shadow & Cliff Lakes: 1.7mi/2.7km one way; allow 2-2.5 hrs.; easy going, strenuous coming back; 800' descent; trailhead: Road Guide Marker #27. This higher-elevation hike is good in late summer when the lakes have warmed for enjoyable swimming. The lakes are small but beautiful. Ranger-conducted hikes are available most years during summer months (check schedule in Lassen Guide).

Kings Creek Falls: 1.2mi/1.9km one way; allow 2 hrs.; easy; 600' descent; trailhead: Road Guide Marker #32. This very pleasant hike leads through a beautiful forest dotted with wildflowers to the Park's second highest waterfall (50 ft.). It is a good hike for small children, elderly, or not-in-such-good-shape adults. (That just about covers everybody.)

Hikes out of Manzanita Lake

Manzanita Creek: 3.5mi/5.7km one way; allow 3.5-4 hrs.; 1200' ascent; trailhead: South end of Manzanita Campground near exit of Loop F. This is a nice hike if the short trails around Manzanita and Reflection Lakes do not offer enough exercise. The trail has a gradual ascent all the way to its conclusion, when it gradually peters out in a mountain meadow. There are many varieties of wildflowers along the way. For the vigorous, experienced hikers, the hike may be extended by following animal trails up Crescent Cliffs to Soda Lake.

Hikes out of Drakesbad

Drakesbad is located approximately 18 miles from Chester, CA on a partially-paved road. Trailers are not recommended from Park Boundary.

Devils Kitchen: 5.6mi/9.0km round trip; allow 3-3.5 hrs.; easy to moderate; 400' ascent; trailhead: parking lot west of Warner Valley Campground. The nearly-level trail passes through a beautiful forest of white fir, Jeffrey pine, and incense cedar before descending into Devils Kitchen. This hydro-thermal area was named for its bubbling mud pots and fumaroles, a portion of which resemble an in-use kitchen stove.

Terminal Geyser: 5.4mi/8.6km round trip; allow 3-3.5 hr.; moderate; 400' ascent; trailhead: parking lot west of Warner Valley Campground. Initially this hike goes to Boiling Springs Lake (a self-guiding nature trail). The trail continues through a beautiful forest to Terminal Geyser (actually a fumarole). Return can be made by a fork to the right .2 miles back from the geyser to initiate a loop return.

Hikes out of Juniper Lake

This area is approximately 16 miles on a partially-paved road from Chester, CA.

Mt. Harkness return on its west side and south side of Juniper Lake: 1.9mi/3.1km to Mt. Harkness, 5.5mi/8.9km for loop; allow 3-3.5 hours.; strenuous; 1400' ascent; trailhead: Juniper Lake Campground. This hike to the Mt. Harkness Lookout provides a fabulous view of the eastern part of the Park and the surrounding area. The return is through interesting rock formations and along the south side of Juniper Lake.

Crystal Lake: .8mi/1.3km round trip; allow .5 hour; moderate; 400' ascent; trailhead: .3 mi. north of the campground on the road towards the Ranger

Station. This is a short but very steep trail to what is considered one of Lassen Park's most beautiful lakes. Take plenty of film and enjoy the swimming, fishing, and scenery. It's a delightful place for a picnic.

Snag Lake return via Horseshoe Lake: 6.9mi/11.2km; allow 4-4.5 hrs.; moderate; 1000' descent then ascent; trailhead: Juniper Lake Ranger Station. This trail is through the heart of the eastern portion of the Park. It offers many variations for backpacking trips to Butte Cluster, Summit, and Twin Lakes. It's a good hike to "get the feel" of Lassen.

Hikes out of Butte Lake

Widow Lake: 3.6mi/5.8km one way; allow 4-4.5 hrs.; moderate; 800' ascent; trailhead: Butte Lake parking area, .2mi. east of the Ranger Station. This trail skirts the east side of Butte Lake, then ascends moderately to steeply for approximately 1.5 miles to Widow Lake. The Lake is a beautiful turquoise color with a grassy edge that provides a nice footing to walk around.

Cinder Cone: 1.9mi/3.0km to the top; allow 2.5 hrs round trip; moderate; 1000' ascent; trailhead: Butte Lake Ranger Station. This self-guiding nature trail ascends 700 vertical feet to a nearly perfect cinder cone. From the rim top, there are impressive panoramic views in all directions. The trail descends into the crater. Climbing out, the trail continues down the south side of the cone, returning via a loop. Or you may return the same way you came, which is shorter.

BRIEF HISTORY

The first humans in the area were the Native American tribes of the Yana, Yahi, Maidu and the Atsugewi. Ishi, the last surviving Indian of the Yana, wandered

half-starved into the town of Oroville, CA in 1911. It seems ironic that long after the Plains and Southwest Indians had been subdued, the last American Indian "to come in" was from such a little-known, comparatively peaceful tribe.

Early explorers named Lassen Peak San José, St. Joseph, Sister Buttes, Lassen Butte, Snow Mountain, Snow Butte, and, in recent times, Mt. Lassen. The current name is named after Peter Lassen, a Danish blacksmith, who emigrated to Northern California. He obtained a Mexican land grant near the present site of Vina, where he founded a town called Benton City. He guided other emigrants over his own Lassen Trail in order to insure that they would arrive at Benton City to buy necessary items to re-supply. He moved to the Honey Lake region and was killed by parties unknown near Black Rock, Nevada, in November 1859.

In 1905 President Theodore Roosevelt established Lassen Peak Forest and, two years later, Lassen Peak and Cinder Cone were made National Monuments. Congressman John Raker, along with local businessmen Arthur L. Conard and Michael E. Dittmar, worked toward the establishment of a national park as early as 1912. Their efforts met with indifference until the eruptions of Lassen Peak in 1914 and 1915. These eruptions focused national attention on Lassen Peak and culminated with the establishment of the Park on August 19, 1916.

The Park has been expanded over the years from its original size of 79,561 acres to its present size of 106,000 acres. In 1974 the visitor facilities (excepting the campground) at Manzanita Lake were closed due to the threat of a rock slide avalanche. Efforts are now being made to re-establish a visitor center at a new location outside the hazard area.

AUTHOR'S COMMENTS

Lassen is my home. I've lived in Mineral for over 30 years. I've hiked every trail twice and some many more times than that. The trails in the eastern part of the Park are so uncrowded that you're glad to meet someone on the trail. It's beautiful country. Some people say I'm prejudiced and, you know, they're probably right.

Mesa Verde

LOCATION: Southwestern Colorado

ACCESS: Midway between Cortez on the west and Mancos on the east on Highway 160.

SEASON: All year

HOURS: Main Park road open 24 hrs/day; Wetherill Mesa Road open a week after Memorial Day to Labor Day; side roads open at 8:00 a.m. but not open during winter following snowfall over several inches

ENTRANCE FEES: $5/vehicle/week; $2/person all others/week; $15 annual; $25 Golden Eagle

GAS & FOOD: Morefield Campground; Far View Terrace

NEAREST PROPANE: Highway 160 east of Park

CAMPGROUND: Morefield Campground (May 1 to October 31)

LODGING: Far View Lodge (view of 4 states!): May-October; 150 rooms; restaurant; bar; reservations: Mesa Verde Company, Box 277, Mancos, CO 81328; 303/529-4421

ADJACENT FACILITIES: Full commercial facilities in Mancos and Cortez; see Adjacent Facilities section for campgrounds

VISITOR CENTER: Far View Visitor Center (summer only)

MUSEUM: Park Headquarters area (year round)

PICNICKING: Museum area; Wetherill Mesa; Ruins Road

GIFT SHOPS: Morefield Campground; Far View Terrace; Far View Lodge; Spruce Tree Terrace (mid-May to mid-October)

TOURS: Ranger-guided tours of 1-3 cliff dwellings year round (weather permitting); self-guided tours to 2 other cliff dwellings and several surface sites

ACTIVITIES: Limited hiking (2 hikes require permit); biking (rentals); bus trips; interpretive programs

CLIMATE: Comfortable in summer; cold with snow in winter

ELEVATION: 6,964 to 8,572 ft. (6,000 ft. in deepest canyon in Park but not open to public)

SIZE: 81 sq. miles

ANNUAL VISITATION: Approximately three-quarters million

PETS: Permitted on leash, except in public buildings and on trails

FACILITIES FOR DISABLED: Morefield Campground; Far View; Chapin Mesa

INFORMATION: *Supt. Mesa Verde National Park*
Mesa Verde National Park, CO 81330
303/529-4465

CAMPGROUND

Morefield Campground: This is the Park's only campground and is located 3 miles from the entrance station. It has 477 sites for both tents and trailers, 17 group camp sites,and 4 sites accessible to physically impaired.It is open from May 1 to mid-October. The fee is $6 per night and limit of stay is 14 days with check-out time of 2:00 p.m. Group camp fee is $1 per person with $10 min. Some sites with electricity are $11 per day for 2 persons plus $2 for each additional person.

The Campground features modern comfort stations, tables and fireplaces at each site,and a sanitary dump station open late May to mid-September. Coin-operated showers and laundry facilities are located at nearby Morefield Village as well as a store, gas station, refreshment center and curio shop. Wood gathering is prohibited in the Park but wood is for sale at the store. Interpretive programs are held at 9 p.m. during the summer months in the amphitheatre located in the Campground.

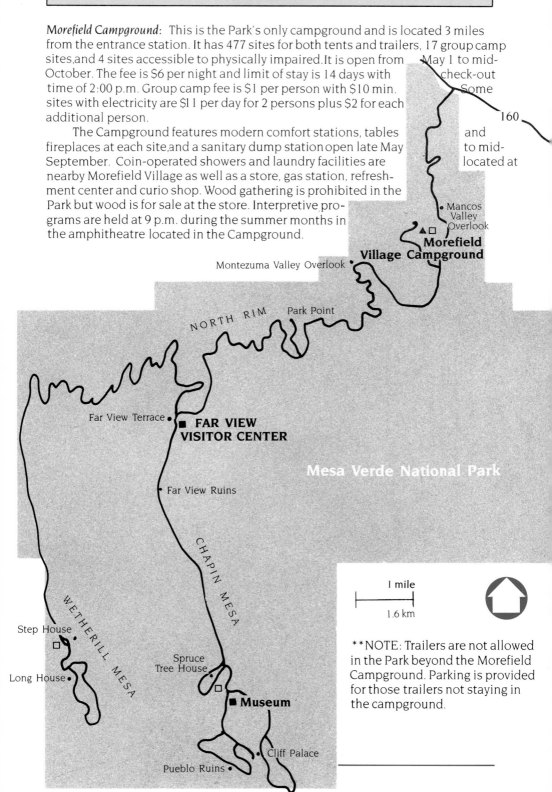

160

Mancos
Valley
Overlook

**Morefield
Village Campground**

Montezuma Valley Overlook •

NORTH RIM   Park Point

Far View Terrace • ■ **FAR VIEW
VISITOR CENTER**

Mesa Verde National Park

• Far View Ruins

CHAPIN MESA

WETHERILL MESA

Step House
□

Long House •

Spruce
Tree House •

□

■ **Museum**

• Cliff Palace

Pueblo Ruins •

1 mile
├────────┤
1.6 km

**NOTE: Trailers are not allowed in the Park beyond the Morefield Campground. Parking is provided for those trailers not staying in the campground.

Motels: Mancos and Cortez

Campgrounds:

Mesa Verde Pt Kampark: ¾ mi. E of entrance on Hwy. 160; open 4/1–11/1; full hook-ups; showers; store; propane

Double A CG & RV Park: 10 mi. E of Cortez on Hwy. 160; open 4/1–11/1; full hook-ups; showers; store

Tiki Verde MHP: ½ mi. W of Mancos; open all year; full hook-ups; showers; propane

Mesa Oasis CG: 4 mi. S of Cortez on Hwy. 160 & 666; open all year; full hook-ups; showers; store

KOA: 1 mi. E of Cortez on Hwy. 160; open 4/15–10/15; full hook-ups; showers; store; propane

AUTHOR'S COMMENTS

Mesa Verde is the only national park which was established not because of the splendors of nature but to preserve the works of man.

HIKING

Chapin Mesa Area

Spruce Tree House Trail: .5mi/.8km round trip; allow 1 hour; trailhead: behind the Museum. This is a self-guiding trail in summer, Ranger-guided trail in winter. This relatively easy and very pleasant trail descends 200 feet to the third largest complex of dwellings.

Petrograph Point Trail: 2.8mi/4.5km round trip; allow 2 hours; trailhead: off the Spruce Tree House Trail. This is a self-guiding trail but hikers must register at the Chief Ranger's office before taking the hike. This is a neat trail best taken early in the morning. The trail is mostly level and proceeds below the edge of the plateau. It climbs up and down narrow rock stairs and squeezes between massive rocks with a view of Spruce Canyon always present. It's not hard to think back hundreds of years and, in the quiet of early morning, in solitude, think of yourself as an Anasazi Indian going after his morning meal. At point number 24 is the climax of the hike, namely, the Anasazi petrographs. The trail terminates at the Museum parking lot.

Spruce Canyon Trail: 2.1mi/3.4km round trip; allow 2 hours; trailhead: the Spruce Tree House. Hikers must register at the Chief Ranger's office. This trail proceeds to the bottom of Spruce Canyon and terminates at the picnic area.

Soda Canyon Overlook: .75mi/1.2km; allow 45 minutes; trailhead: at a turnout approximately .75 miles north of Balcony House. This level trail through a juniper forest provides overlooks of Soda Canyon and Balcony House and is an excellent place for photographing Balcony House.

Balcony House Trail: .5mi/.8km round trip; allow 1 hour; open May–Sept.; trailhead: Ruins Loop Road. This Ranger-guided tour views the Balcony House Ruins.

Cliff Palace Trail: .5mi/.8km round trip; allow 1 hour; trailhead: the Cliff Palace parking area. The trail descends steeply into the largest complex of cliff dwellings.

Far View Area

Far View Ruin Self-guiding Trail: 1.0mi/1.6km round trip; allow 1 hour. This level, easy trail winds through surface ruins, which may be climbed for closer inspection.

Wetherill Mesa Area

• The area is open from early June through Labor Day.
• The road is open to private vehicular travel (limited to 22 ft). Private cars will park at the concession area and take the mini train to Long House, Long House Overlook, Kodak House Overlook, and to visit 4 mesa-top sites in the Badger House Community·
• Allow one hour each way for travel to Wetherill Mesa.

Long House Ruin Trail: .75mi/1.2km round trip; allow 2 hours; trailhead: the end of the mini-bus ride. This Ranger-guided tour descends steeply into the Ruin.

Step House Ruin Self-Guided Trail: .5mi/.8km round trip; allow 45 minutes; trailhead: the parking lot. This trail is very steep and tours Pit House and cliff dwellings of two different periods in time.

Morefield Area

Prater Ridge Trail: 7.8mi/12.5km loop; allow 4 hours; trailhead: west side of Morefield Campground. The trail ascends the east side of Prater Ridge, follows a loop around the top, and returns.

Knife Edge Trail: 3.0mi/4.8km round trip; allow 2 hours. The trail follows the old road alignment from Morefield Campground to Montezuma Valley Overlook, which is a good place from which to watch sunsets.

Point Lookout Trail: 2.3mi/3.7km round trip; allow 2 hours. This nature trail switchbacks up Point Lookout and follows along the mesa. The trail provides excellent views of Mancos and Montezuma Valleys.

BRIEF HISTORY

The history of Mesa Verde is basically the history of the Anasazi Indians. They arrived around A.D. 550 and were highly-skilled basket makers. Originally they lived in pit houses and, as time progressed, so did their skills. The bow and arrow replaced the atlatl (a spear thrower). Pottery was developed. And starting around A.D. 750, pueblos were constructed. These eventually evolved into apartments, the ruins of which we view today.

The Anasazi civilization reached its zenith in the twelfth century and then, suddenly, the Indians disappeared from Mesa Verde. They left their homes as though they expected to return within hours. Scientists do not know exactly where they went or why they left.

The first white settlers in the area were Benjamen Weatherill and his family. On December 18, 1888, while chasing stray cattle in a snowstorm, his sons and a son-in-law discovered Cliff Palace. The Weatherills shared their find with the world, selling artifacts until 1895 when they realized the historic significance of their discovery.

Unsuccessful efforts in 1891 and 1894 were made by the Colorado legislature to the United States Congress to preserve Mesa Verde as a national park. However, efforts continued and President Theodore Roosevelt signed a bill establishing the Park on June 29, 1906.

Mt. Rainier

LOCATION:	Southwestern Washington
ACCESS:	Hwy. 410 from north and east; Hwy. 123 from south; Hwy. 706 from west
SEASON:	All year; only road plowed from late Nov. to June is from Nisqually Entrance to Paradise
HOURS:	24 hours/day
ENTRANCE FEES:	$5/vehicle/week; $2/person all others/week; $15 annual; $25 Golden Eagle
FOOD:	In summer, at Longmire, Paradise, Sunrise; in winter, restaurant daily at Longmire and snack bar on weekends and holidays at Paradise
GAS:	Longmire
NEAREST PROPANE:	Ashford (10 mi. W); Packwood (11 mi. S)
CAMPGROUNDS:	Major summer season campgrounds at Ohanapecosh, White River and Cougar Rock; Sunshine Point (Nisqually Entrance) open all year; no hook-ups; numerous backcountry camps (permit required 6/15–9/30)
LODGING:	National Park Inn at Longmire (all year); Paradise Inn (summer only)—see below
ADJACENT FACILITIES:	Numerous motels, trailer parks, a hotel and housekeeping cabins near Park boundaries
VISITOR CENTERS:	Longmire (all year); Paradise (daily May-Dec., weekends & holidays Jan.-Apr.); Ohanapecosh (late May-Oct.); Sunrise (July-Sept.)
MUSEUM:	Longmire
PICNICKING:	At designated areas throughout Park
GIFT SHOPS:	Paradise Inn and Visitor Center; National Park Inn; Sunrise Lodge
TOURS:	Naturalist-led walks
ACTIVITIES:	Hiking; rock and ice climbing w/school & equipment rentals available (regulated by NPS—write Supt. for information); backpacking; horseback riding (on designated trails only— no rentals); fishing; winter sports; interpretive programs
CLIMATE:	Changeable weather; warm days mid-summer to fall; heavy snow in winter
ELEVATION:	1,914 to 14,410 ft.
SIZE:	378 sq. miles
ANNUAL VISITATION:	Approximately two million
PETS:	Must be on leash; not allowed on trails or in public buildings

FACILITIES FOR DISABLED: Most public buildings; some restrooms

INFORMATION: Supt. Mt. Rainier National Park
Tahoma Woods, Star Route
Ashford, WA 98304
206/569-2211

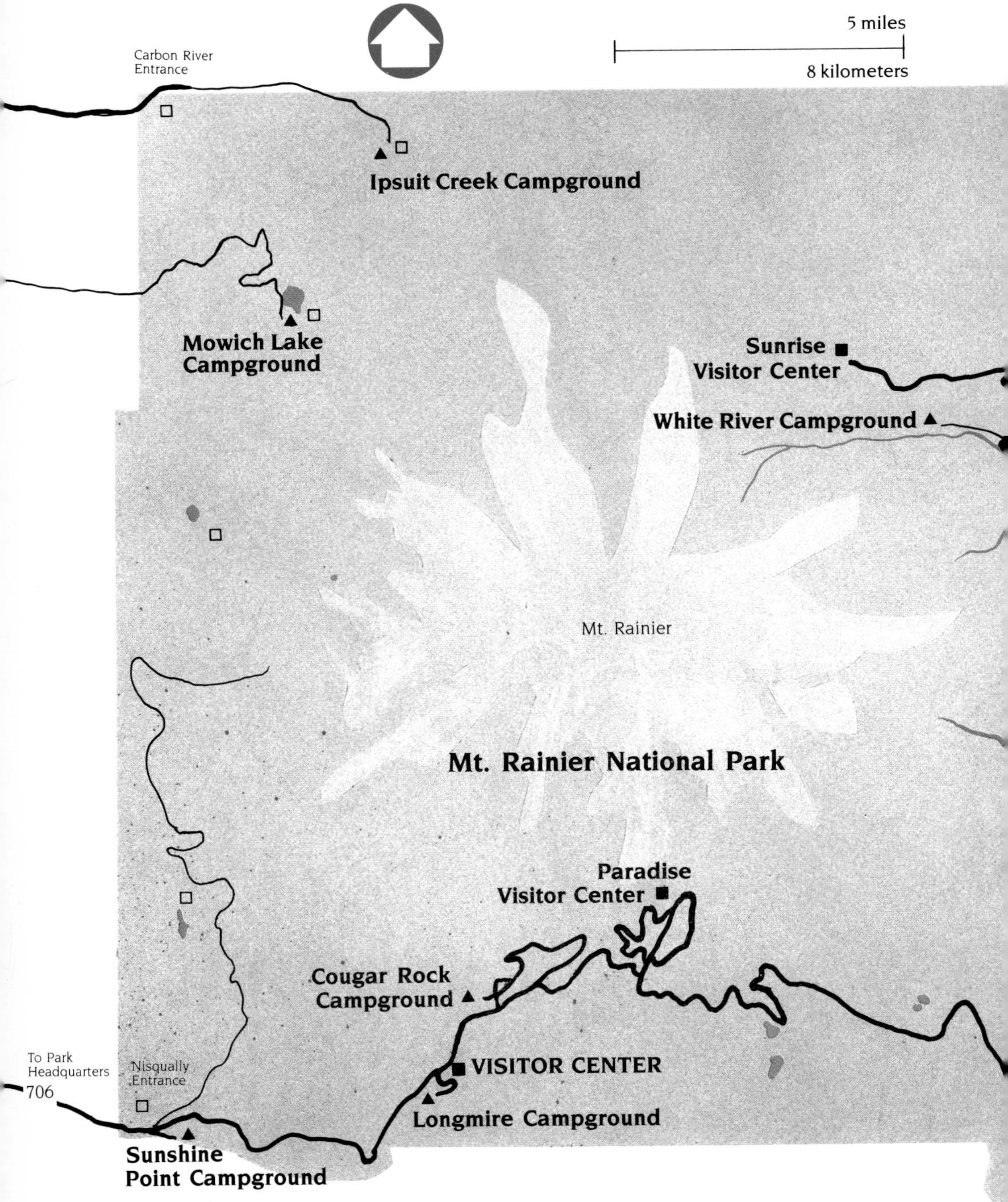

5 miles

8 kilometers

Carbon River
Entrance

Ipsuit Creek Campground

**Mowich Lake
Campground**

**Sunrise ■
Visitor Center**

White River Campground ▲

Mt. Rainier

Mt. Rainier National Park

**Paradise
Visitor Center ■**

**Cougar Rock
Campground ▲**

To Park
Headquarters
706

Nisqually
Entrance

■ VISITOR CENTER

Longmire Campground

**Sunshine
Point Campground**

- Stated camping season of each campground is approximate depending on the weather (except Sunshine Point open year round).
- All individual campsites include nearby piped drinking water, fireplace, a table/bench combination, and are on a first-come basis.
- Group campsites include multiple tent-site area with central fireplace and scattered table/bench combinations and reservations are accepted up to 90 days in advance: Chief Ranger, Mt. Rainier Nat'l Park, Tahoma Woods, Star Route, Ashford, WA 98304. The fee is $1/person, $12 minimum.
- A $2 fee is charged for extra vehicle at all campsites.
- Wood-gathering is prohibited except dead and down in river beds at Sunshine Point and Ipsut Creek; wood is for sale at Longmire Service Station, Stagecoach and White River Campgrounds.
- Campsites have a 14-day limit of stay mid-June through Labor Day, a 30-day limit of stay rest of year.
- There are no trailer hook-ups in the Park.
- Public showers are located at Paradise Visitor Center.
- There are no laundry facilities in the Park.
- Ice is available at Longmire.
- Interpretive programs are conducted during summer months at campground amphitheaters except Sunshine Point.

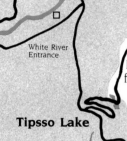

410

White River
Entrance

Tipsso Lake

Ohanapecosh
Campground
VISITOR CENTER

Stevens Canyon
Entrance

Cougar Rock (elev. 3180') is located 8 mi. NE of Nisqually Entrance. It has 200 individual sites, 5 group sites, and is open June-Oct. The fee is $5 per night. Facilities include flush toilets, an amphitheater, dump station, ranger station, and a restroom for handicapped.

Longmire is strictly an overflow campground for Cougar Rock. It has 60 sites *for tents only* and is open June-Oct. Facilities include flush toilets.

Ipsut Creek (elev. 2300') is located 5 mi. E of Carbon River Entrance. It has 30 individual sites, 2 group sites, and is open May-Nov. but often in winter as well with no water. The fee is $4 per night. Facilities include pit toilets, an amphitheater, and a self-guided trail. The campground is useable by handicapped.

Ohanapecosh (elev. 1914') is located 1-1½ mi. S of Stevens Canyon Entrance. It has 232 individual sites with 30 riverfront sites and is open June-Nov. The fee is $5 per night and $6 per night for riverfront sites. Facilities include flush toilets, an amphitheater, visitor center, self-guided trail, and a dump station.

Sunshine Point (elev. 2000') is located ⅓ mi. E of Nisqually Entrance in an open, grassy area adjacent to the Nisqually River. It has 18 individual sites and is open all year. Facilities include pit toilets, and the fee is $4 per night. The campground is useable by the handicapped.

White River (elev. 4400') is located 5 mi. W of White River Entrance in a heavily-wooded area of fir and cedar. It has 117 sites and is open July-Oct. Facilities include flush toilets, and the fee is $5 per night. The campground has a small amphitheater.

Mowich Lake (elev. 4950') is located near the shores of Mowich Lake. It has 25 sites and is a *hike-into, tents-only* campground. Facilities include pit toilets and a ranger station.

Backcountry Camping (Overnight permit required)

There are three different kinds of backcountry camping experiences available. These include established *trailside camps*, which have toilet facilities, nearby water source and marked areas in which to set up camp; *crosscountry camping*, whereby you choose your own campsite out of sight of trails and a minimum of 100 ft. from lakes and streams; *alpine camping*, which is camping above 7000 ft. on the snow or at designated areas; no open fires are allowed.

ACCOMMODATIONS

Paradise Inn: On Park Road at Paradise; open Memorial Day weekend to October; 127 rooms, most with private baths; dining room; lounge; gift shop; snack bar.

National Park Inn: On Park Road at Longmire; open year-round; 16 rooms, 8 with private baths; dining room; country store.

For Reservations: Mt. Rainier Guest Services, Attn: Reservations, 55106 Kernahan Rd. E, Ashford, WA 98304; 206/569-2275

HIKING

There are over 300 miles of trails in the Park. Detailed information is available by writing the Park Superintendent or at visitor centers, most ranger stations, and hiker information centers (open daily mid-June to Sept. at Longmire and White River).

Hiking Mt. Rainier: See above for detailed information. A free permit is required for overnight hikes. A climbing card is required for climbing the mountain above Camp Muir or Camp Schurman.

SELF-GUIDING NATURE HIKES

At Paradise

Nisqually Vista Trail: 1.2mi/1.9km; allow 1 hour; descent 200'; trailhead: in parking lot of Visitor Center. This trail tells the story of how weather shapes the landscape and features good views of Mt. Rainier and Nisqually Glacier.

At Longmire

Trail of the Shadows: 0.5mi/0.8km; 30 minutes; trailhead: across the highway from National Park Inn. This mostly level trail leads around Longmire Meadow and features the natural environment and a step back into history with the remnants of the Longmire Hotel.

At Carbon River

Carbon River Rain Forest: 0.3mi/0.5km; 20 minutes; trailhead: right side of road at Park Entrance. This mostly level trail explores a rain forest that is unique because of its distance from the coastal area.

At Sunrise

Sourdough Ridge Trail: 0.5mi/0.8km; 30 minutes; trailhead: N side of picnic area. Walk through flower fields with views of mountain peaks on this trail.

At Ohanapecosh

Life System: 0.5mi/0.8km; 30 minutes. This trail explores both forest and hot springs.

Grove of the Patriarchs: 1.5mi/2.3km round trip; 1 hour; trailhead: parking lot beyond Ohanapecosh River Bridge on Stevens Canyon Road. This mostly level trail leads through an old growth forest of huge Douglas firs, western hemlock and western red cedar.

From Paradise

Lakes Trail: 5.0mi/8.0km loop; 4 hours; easy; ascent 700'; trailhead: across the road from Paradise Inn or stone steps left of restrooms. Numerous lakes including Reflection Lake, meadows of wildflowers, mountain vistas, and lush forest mantle are some features of this gentle up-and-down trail.

Lakes High Trail: 4.0mi/6.4km loop; 3 hours; easy. This shortened version of the Lakes Trail offers views of wildlife and a variety of wildflowers.

Skyline Trail: 5.0mi/8.0km loop; 4 hours; moderate; ascent 1700'; trailhead: in front of Paradise Inn or stone steps left of restrooms. On a clear day, Mt. Hood,

100 miles away in Oregon, can be seen from this trail. Other features include the Nisqually Glacier with its avalanches and panoramic vistas of Paradise Valley, Mt. Adams and Mt. St. Helens.

Golden Gate Trail: 4.0mi/6.4km loop; 3 hours; moderate. This shortened version of the Skyline Trail offers views of wildflowers in the Edith Creek basin.

Alta Vista Trail: 1.5mi/2.4km loop; 1 hour; easy; ascent 500'; trailheads: from Visitor Center, Paradise Inn or Ranger Station. This steep loop leads through spectacular wildflowers to a green knoll above Paradise Valley with views of Mt. Adams and Mt. St. Helens, and Mt. Hood visible between the two on a clear day.

Moraine Trail: 3.0mi/4.8km round trip; 1.75 hours; easy; ascent 600'; trailhead: Visitor Center. This little-hiked trail with its profusion of wildflowers is ideal for those wishing solitude along with beauty. Sturdy boots are recommended because of the rocky terraine.

Ice Caves Trail: 6.0mi/9.6km round trip; 5 hours; trailhead: Visitor Center. This trail merges with the Skyline Trail before continuing through an area recently shaped by glacial ice and proceeds to the Ice Caves. The Caves may be buried in snow; check with a ranger.

From Carbon River

Paul Peak Loop: 7.5mi/12.0km round trip; 3 hours; moderate; ascent 800'; trailhead: Paul Peak picnic area. This gentle trail features a lush silent forest and waterfall mists. It's an ideal walk when higher trails are still snowbound.

Tolmie Peak: 6.5mi/10.4km round trip; 3 hours; moderate; ascent 1010'; trailhead: left side of road at Mowich Lake. Observing the meadows around Eunice Lake, one of the prettiest lakes in the park, and viewing Mt. Rainier across its shores highlight the many features of this trail.

Spray Park: 6.0mi/9.6km round trip; 3 hours; moderate; ascent 1050'; trailhead: parking lot at west side of Mowich Lake. Many hikers claim this as their favorite trail with its roaming meadows, quiet ponds, sparkling falls, breathtaking glacier-views, gentle ridges for exploring, and, in particular, its spectacular array of wildflowers.

Listed below are a few popular day hikes.

From Longmire

Eagle Peak Saddle: 7.0mi/11.2km round trip; 5 hours; strenuous; ascent 2955'; trailhead: 200 ft. from suspension bridge over Nisqually River. This trail provides a gentle grade over a well-marked trail until the last half mile of a steep and rocky climb to the saddle, where the hiker is treated to panoramic views of Mt. Rainier and surrounding mountain ranges, farms, and forests.

Rampart Ridge: 4.5mi/7.2km loop; 2.5 hours; moderate; ascent 1800'; trailhead: left segment of Trail of the Shadows nature walk across from National Park Inn. This loop trail ascends through forest to spectacular vistas of the Nisqually Valley along the cliffs and is best taken clockwise for glimpses of Mt. Rainier along the way.

Kautz Creek: 11.0mi/17.6km round trip; 6 hours; strenuous; ascent 2300'; trailhead: across highway from parking area near nature exhibit at the Kautz Creek bridge. This trail provides virgin forest, high meadow country, and superb mountain views on its gentle climb to Indian Henry's Hunting Ground.

From Sunrise

Burroughs Mountain: 7.0mi/11.2km round trip; 3 hours; moderate; ascent 900'; trailhead: North side of parking area. Spectacular close-up views of Mt. Rainier, late-summer wildflowers and a rest stop at the memorial to Edmond S. Meany, past President of The Mountaineers, are some of the features of this trail. Burroughs Mountain is an extremely fragile alpine area; hikers must stay on the trails to avoid damaging the resource.

Mount Fremont: 5.5mi/8.8km round trip; 3 hours; moderate; ascent 1200'; trailhead: 1.5 miles west from Sunrise parking area on Wonderland Trail. On a clear day, hikers are afforded views of Mt. Rainier, the Cascades and the Olympics on their way up this moderate trail to the fire lookout.

From White River

Glacier Basin: 6.6mi/10.6km round trip; 4 hours; moderate; ascent 1280'; trailhead: upper end of campground. Park in day-use parking lot. A diversion from this trail at 1 mile leads to a viewpoint overlooking Emmons Glacier, the largest glacier in the contiguous U.S. Other features include meadows of wildflowers and possible views of mountain goats.

Summerland: 8.5mi/13.6km round trip; 4 hours; moderate; ascent 1500'; trailhead: across the road from parking area near Fryingpan Creek bridge (3 mi. from White River entrance). This trail offers good views of Mt. Rainier and Little Tahoma, spectacular wildflowers in its upper meadows, and possible sightings of wildlife. It's one of the Park's most popular hikes, and parking at the trailhead is limited, especially on weekends.

From Ohanapecosh

Silver Falls: 3.0mi/4.8km loop; 1.5 hours; easy; ascent 300'; trailhead: on Hot Springs Nature Trail behind Visitor Center. This gentle loop trail ascends the east bank of the Ohanapecosh River to views of Silver Falls and returns via the west side of the valley.

East Side Trail: 9.0mi/14.4km one way; 4 hours; descent 1500'; trailhead: .5 mi. S of Deer Creek. This gentle trail is ideal when the higher trails are still snow-covered or weather conditions are adverse. It descends through forest, above a pretty canyon and over waterfalls, always within sound of the River. Arrange for pick-up at Ohanapecosh, if possible.

BRIEF HISTORY

Native Americans followed the retreating snows of the last Ice Age and occupied the lower elevations of the Pacific Northwest. They journeyed to the higher country as winter snows melted, hunting migrating game. When the white settlers arrived in the 1860's, western Washington was populated by the Cowlit, Nisqually, Klickitat, Yakima and Puyallup Indian tribes.

The Indians' name for the vast snow-covered mountain that dominated the region was Takhoma or Tahoma, "The Mountain". In 1792 Captain George Vancouver of the British navy named "The Mountain" for his friend Admiral Peter Rainier. In 1833 Dr. William Tolmie organized a scientific expedition to explore the mountain. An early settler, James Longmire, made his home and

---

built a resort at the present site of Longmire on the southwest corner of the Park.

In 1870 the first documented ascent of the summit of Mt. Rainier was made by Philemon Van Trump and the appropriately-named Hazard Stevens. Through the years an ever-increasing number of people climb or attempt to climb the mountain. At the present time, approximately 8,000 people attempt to climb and a good number of them succeed. Efforts to establish Mount Rainier as a park started in the early 1890's. Efforts of local newspapers and conservation and scientific organizations succeeded, and Mount Rainier National Park was officially established on March 2, 1899, when President William McKinley signed the bill.

AUTHOR'S COMMENTS

Mount Rainier is impressive. It is used by the locals as a sort of weather barometer—"You can see the mountain today", or perhaps more often, "You can't see the mountain today".

Mt. Rainier is considered an active volcano, part of the "circle of fire", in the Cascade Mountains which extends to Lassen Peak at the southern extreme. Most scientists agree that it will erupt again some time in the future.

For picture-taking, I have a number of suggestions. One, take extra film, for the views of the mountain are constantly changing as you drive or hike through the Park. Two, try to visit on a clear day, as the mountain is often shrouded in clouds. Three, if possible plan your visit to enter the Park from the north (Hwy. 410) in the morning and drive through the Park in a clockwise direction so the sun is at your back.

Mt. Rainier dominates the landscape of the Pacific Northwest. It can be seen for hundreds of miles, and, in the author's opinion, no trip to Washington state would be complete without visiting Mt. Rainier National Park.

North Cascades

LOCATION:	North central Washington
ACCESS:	Washington 20 (North Cascades Highway)
SEASON:	Open all year; North Cascades Highway closed mid-November to mid-April but plowed from west to gate at the trailhead for trail to Ross Dam
HOURS:	24 hours/day
ENTRANCE FEES:	None
FOOD:	Diablo Lake Resort; Stehekin and North Cascades Lodge in Lake Chelan Nat'l Rec. Area; Newhalem; Marblemount
GAS:	Diablo Lake Resort; Ross Lake Resort (boats only); Marblemount
NEAREST PROPANE:	Marblemount
CAMPGROUNDS:	Several along Hwy. 20; numerous only accessible by trail, boat or shuttlebus and require backcountry permit; showers and laundry facilities at Diablo Lake Resort
LODGING:	Diablo Lake Resort; North Cascades Lodge; Ross Lake Resort; Stehekin Valley Ranch; Silver Bay Inn; cabins in Stehekin (see below)
VISITOR CENTERS:	Sedro Woolley Information Center; Early Winters Information Center; Glacier Information Center
PICNICKING:	Throughout the Park
GIFT SHOP:	North Cascades Lodge
TOURS:	Ranger-led walks in summer at Colonial Creek and Newhalem Campgrounds, Hozomeen, and at Stehekin; raft trips year round from Goodell Creek Campground; ski tours in winter at Stehekin; commercial float trips
ACTIVITIES:	Hiking; boating (state license required); fishing (state license required); mountaineering (commercial schools available); horseback riding; cross-country skiing; intrepretive programs
CLIMATE:	Cool and damp west of Cascades; warm days and cool nights on the east
ELEVATION:	350 ft. to 9206 ft.
SIZE:	1,053 sq. mi. including Ross Lake and Lake Chelan Nat'l Recreation Areas
ANNUAL VISITATION:	Approximately three-quarters million
PETS:	Not permitted in Park except on leash on Pacific Crest Trail; permitted on leash in recreational areas
FACILITIES FOR DISABLED:	Most restrooms; lift and ramp at No. Cascades Lodge; campsites and amphitheaters useable

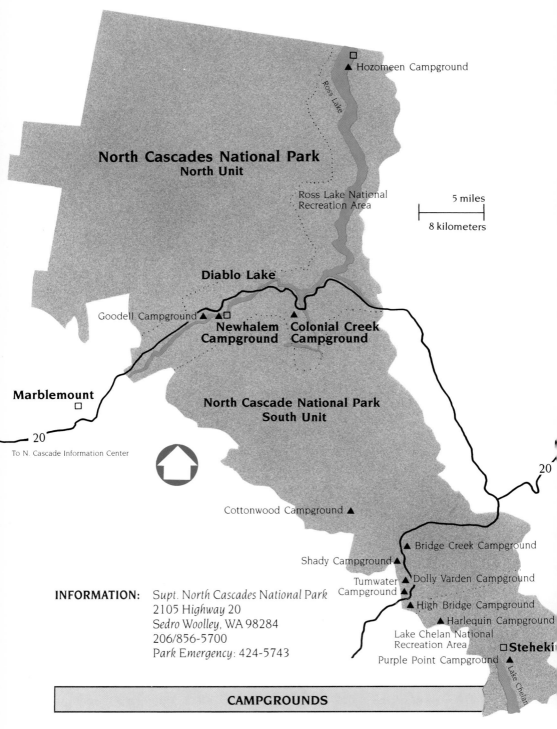

North Cascades National Park
North Unit

Ross Lake

▢
▲ Hozomeen Campground

Ross Lake National Recreation Area

5 miles
8 kilometers

Diablo Lake

Goodell Campground ▲ ▲▢
Newhalem Campground

Colonial Creek Campground
▲

Marblemount
▢

20

To N. Cascade Information Center

North Cascade National Park
South Unit

20

Cottonwood Campground ▲

▲ Bridge Creek Campground

Shady Campground ▲

Tumwater Campground ▲ ▲ Dolly Varden Campground

INFORMATION: Supt. North Cascades National Park
2105 Highway 20
Sedro Woolley, WA 98284
206/856-5700
Park Emergency: 424-5743

▲ High Bridge Campground

▲ Harlequin Campground

Lake Chelan National Recreation Area

▢ Steheki

Purple Point Campground ▲

Lake Chelan

CAMPGROUNDS

Stehekin Valley Campgrounds

The following are the only campgrounds in North Cascades National Park, per se. They are *accessible only by trail or shuttlebus*, and a backcountry camping permit is required. There is no campground fee or limit of stay. The campsites have tables and fireplaces, pit toilets, and fishing is available. Distances given are from Stehekin.

Bridge Creek (16 mi.) has 7 sites, 1 group campsite, and is open May to Oct.

Cottonwood (23 mi.) has 5 sites and is open June to Oct.

Dolly Varden (14 mi.) has 1 site and is open May to Oct.

High Bridge (11 mi.) has 2 sites and is open May to Nov.

Shady (15 mi.) has 1 site and is open May to Oct.

Tumwater (13 mi.) has 2 sites and is open May to Oct.

Ross Lake National Recreation Area Campgrounds
(Administered by National Park Service)

Highway Access Campgrounds

• All campsites are self-registration and on a first-come basis.
• All campsites have tables and fireplaces.
• Dead and down firewood may be gathered except in Colonial Creek, Goodell Creek, Hozomeen, and Newhalem campgrounds.
• There is no limit of stay in the campgrounds.

Colonial Creek (elev. 1200') is located on Hwy. 20, 25 mi. E of Marblemount, in a wooded area on the shores of Diablo Lake. It has 164 sites for tents or large trailers, is open mid-April to Nov. 1, and usually fills on weekends in summer. Facilities include flush toilets and piped water, and the fee is $5 per night. Additional features include a dump station, amphitheater, fish cleaning table, a boat launch, and a self-guiding nature trail. There are some sites and facilities for handicapped in the campground.

Goodell Creek (elev. 500') is located off Hwy. 20, 15 mi. E of Marblemount, in a heavily wooded area adjacent to the Skagit River. It has 22 sites for tents or small trailers and is open all year, although there may be snow on the ground between December and March. Facilities include pit toilets and piped water, and the fee is $3 per night. There's a raft launch area into the Skagit River.

Gorge Lake (elev. 900') is located on Hwy. 20, has 12 sites, and is open all year. Facilities include pit toilets, and there is no campground fee. There's a boat launch area at the campground.

Hozomeen (elev. 1700') is located on Canada 3 near the British Columbia border. It has 122 individual sites and 1 group campsite and is open May 15 to October 31. Facilities include pit toilets, and there is no campground fee. There's a boat launch area at the campground, and fishing is available.

Newhalem (elev. 500') is located on Hwy. 20 14 mi. E of Marblemount and adjacent to the Skagit River. It has 129 sites for tents or trailers including 13 walk-in sites and is open mid-June to Labor Day. Facilities include flush toilets and water, and the fee is $5 per night. Additional features include a dump station, amphitheater, trailheads for several hikes including a nature hike, and fishing. The campground has handicapped access.

Ross Lake and Diablo Lake Trail or Boat Access Campgrounds

There are around 20 campgrounds in the area accessible by trail or boat. These campgrounds have from 1 to 7 sites, some have group sites, and most are open June 1 to Nov. 1 (a few from May 1). A backcountry camping permit is required.

There is no campground fee or limit of stay. Facilities include pit toilets, tables and fireplaces. Most of the campgrounds have boating and fishing available.

ACCOMMODATIONS

Diablo Lake Resort: Open all year; 20 housekeeping cabins of various size; store; lounge; restaurant; marina; reservations: Diablo Lake Resort, Diablo, Rockport, WA 98283; tele. Everett, WA 206 operator, ask for Newhalem 5578

North Cascades Lodge: Accessible only by boat or plane (leave from Chelan) or 11 mi. trail; open all year; 18 lodge rooms and 8 housekeeping cabins; dining room; lounge; gift shop; store; outdoor game area; ski shop; reservations: Box 186, Chelan, WA 98816; Lodge phone: 509/682-4711, ferry phone: 509/682-2224, Chelan Airways phone: 509/682-5555

Ross Lake Resort: Accessible only by boat/truck rides (resort sits above water on log rafts); open mid-Jan. to late Oct.; 8 cabins with baths; 2 rustic cabins; 1 bunkhouse for groups to 10 (all housekeeping); reservations: Ross Lake Resort, Rockport, WA 98283; tele. Everett, WA 206 operator, ask for Newhalem 7735

Stehekin Valley Ranch, Box 36, Stehekin, WA 98852; 509/682-4677

Silver Bay Inn (Bed and Breakfast): Box 43, Stehekin, WA 98852; 509/682-2212 or 662-0151

Cabins For Rent (All Stehekin, WA 98851):
HAMMETT'S MOUNTAIN CABIN, Box 72;
HONEY BEAR BAKERY CABIN, Box 61;
PARK'S PLACE, Box 66;
RAINBOW CABIN, Box 11;
UNIQUE HOUSEKEEPING UNIT, Box 25.

HIKING

There are approximately 300 miles of trails in North Cascades National Park. Trails below 3,000 ft. are open for hiking by mid-April or early May, whereas higher elevation trails may still have snow in July. The 600,000 acres accessible by the trails offer a variety of old-growth forest, valleys, alpine lakes and streams, and of course the crags, peaks, spires and horns of this spectacular mountain range.

Individual trail information can be obtained at any ranger station or information center. A free permit is required for overnight camping.

The following hiking books are usually available for purchase at Sedro Woolley, Early Winters, and Glacier Information Centers:
Sierra Club Tote Book
Hiking the North Cascades by Fred T. Darvill, Jr.
100 Hikes in the North Cascades by Ira Spring & Harvey Manning
Softly in the Wilderness by John Hart
Pleasure Packing for the Eighties by Robert S. Wood

There is also a catalogue available entitled "Books and Maps North Cascades National Park" published by the Pacific Northwest Nat'l Parks and Forests Association.

BRIEF HISTORY

Originally the Native Americans, a number of tribes, used the area as a summer home. But there were no permanent villages. The first prominent white explorer was Alexander Ross who, in 1814, tried unsuccessfully to find a westward route to Puget Sound. Henry Custer, a topographer, was assigned in 1859 to survey the American-Canadian boundary and explored the northern boundary area of the park. He wrote of the spectacular scenery of his explorations. "It must be seen— it cannot be described."

Mining occurred from the 1880's to 1950, but due partially to the rugged mountainous terrain, it was, for the most part, unsuccessful. Logging continued mainly in the lower elevations up to 1969.

The hydroelectric potential of the area was recognized as early as 1905, and in 1919, construction began on the first of three dams: the Gorge, Diablo and Ross. Then, in 1947, the project was completed. The towns of Newhalem and Diablo were born during construction of the dams and survive in the present for the maintenance and operational phase of the project.

As early as the 1890's conservationists desired a national park to preserve the awesome wilderness of the North Cascade range. However, it wasn't until October 2, 1968 that the Park was established. North Cascades Highway (WA 20) was completed in 1972. It is considered the most scenic mountain drive in the state.

AUTHOR'S COMMENTS

North Cascades National Park is bisected by the Ross Lake National Recreation Area into a north and south unit. Washington Highway 20 runs east and west through the Ross Lake Recreational unit. Lake Chelan National Recreation Area consists of a portion bordering the south unit, and all four areas are administered by the National Park Service. For most visitors, Hwy. 20 serves as the gateway to the Park. The mountains themselves know no political boundaries, and they are enjoyed equally well from national park, forest or recreational areas.

Olympic

LOCATION: Northwestern Washington, Olympic Peninsula

ACCESS: U.S. 101 main access; ferry system/Hood Canal Bridge and air service from Seattle

SEASON: All year, but some main roads closed by snow in winter months

HOURS: 24 hours/day

ENTRANCE FEES: $3/vehicle/week; $1/person all others/week; $9/annual park-specific permit (all collected at Heart O' the Hills, Soleduck and the Hoh from Memorial Day through Labor Day, or later); $25 Golden Eagle

FOOD: Kalaloch Lodge; Lake Crescent Lodge; Log Cabin Resort; Sol Duc Hot Springs Resort; Hurricane Ridge Lodge (day use only—weekends in winter); Fairholm Visitor Service Area

GAS: Fairholm Visitor Service Area; Kalaloch Lodge

NEAREST PROPANE: Port Angeles

CAMPGROUNDS: Numerous throughout park; some open all year; trailer sites best accommodate vehicles to 21 feet but a few in all major campgrounds will accommodate up to 35 ft.

LODGING: Kalaloch Lodge; Log Cabin Resort; Lake Crescent Lodge; Sol Duc Hot Springs Resort (see below for reservation information) NOTE: Because of the Park's proximity to the greater Seattle metropolitan area, the Park's facilities are much less crowded during the week

ADJACENT FACILITIES: Numerous commercial facilities; for information, write Olympic Peninsula Travel Association, P.O. Box 625, Port Angeles, WA 98362 (ask for "Olympic Peninsula Directory") or Olympic Peninsula Resort and Hotel Assoc., Coleman Ferry Bldg., Seattle, WA 98104

VISITOR CENTERS: Pioneer Memorial Museum in Port Angeles; Hoh Rain Forest Visitor Center (both year round); Storm King Ranger Station at Lake Crescent (seasonal); a small visitor center in Hurricane Ridge Lodge; Kalaloch Visitor Center (summers)

MUSEUM: Pioneer Memorial Museum (Port Angeles)

PICNICKING: Designated sites throughout Park; Rialto Beach outside Park

GIFT SHOP: Sol Duc Hot Springs Resort; Hurricane Ridge Lodge

TOURS: Commercial charter bus in summer

ACTIVITIES: Hiking; mountaineering; fishing; boating (rentals available); swimming; water skiing; horseback riding; cross-country and alpine skiing (rentals and instruction available); interpretive programs; field seminars (brochure available—contact Olympic Field Seminars c/o Olympic NP)

CLIMATE:	Cool and sunny with rain in summer; extremely wet in winter with snow at higher elevations; 4 distinct areas, with average rainfall of 24.6″ at Port Angeles, 100.25″ at Staircase (Lake Cushman), 121.10″ at Kalaloch (Ocean Beaches) and 133.58″ at Hoh (Rain Forest)
ELEVATION:	Sea level to 7,965 ft.
SIZE:	Approximately 916,136 acres
ANNUAL VISITATION:	Nearly three million
PETS:	Must be on leash; not allowed on trails, in the backcountry, or public buildings
FACILITIES FOR DISABLED:	All visitor centers; Pioneer Memorial Museum
INFORMATION:	*Supt. Olympic National Park* *600 East Park Ave.* *Port Angeles,* WA 98362 206/452-4501

*NOTE: The Sol Duc Road and Lodge and Soleduck Campground will be closed from October 1968 to May 1988 for road reconstruction.

CAMPGROUNDS

• All campsites are on a first-come basis with a 14-day limit of stay.
• Individual campsites provide tables and grills.
• All campgrounds have modern comfort stations and piped water except Boulder Creek, Deer Park, Erickson's Bay, North Fork, and Ozette.
• All fees are $5 per night except where indicated by ''*'', where there is no fee.
• Trailer sites best accommodate trailers to 21 ft.
• There are no hook-ups, showers, or laundry facilities in the national park campgrounds. (Showers are available at Sequim Bay State Park, Bogachiel State Park, and Dosewallips State Park; laundry facilities are available in Port Angeles, Sequim, La Push, Forks and some smaller towns along Hwy. 101.)
• There are 2 concessioner-operated trailer parks with electricity and water hook-ups: Sol Duc Hot Springs (dump station nearby) and Log Cabin Resort (laundromat)
• Dead and down firewood may be collected below 3500′ unless specifically prohibited.
• There are group campsites at Kalaloch, Mora and Ozette Campgrounds; contact Park Headquarters or the respective ranger station for reservations.
• Fishing is available at all campgrounds except Deer Park and Heart O' The Hills.
• Interpretive programs are conducted in amphitheaters July through Labor Day.

Altaire (elev. 450′) is located 13 miles west of Port Angeles in a shaded, level area on the Elwha River. It has 29 sites and is open June to Sept. The campground has a ranger station nearby.

*Boulder Creek** (elev. 2,060′) is located 20 miles west of Port Angeles. It is a walk-in campground with 50 tents-only sites and is closed when it snows.

*Deer Park** (elev. 5,400′) is located 22 miles southeast of Port Angeles on a dirt road. The campground has 18 sites for tents only and is closed when it snows.

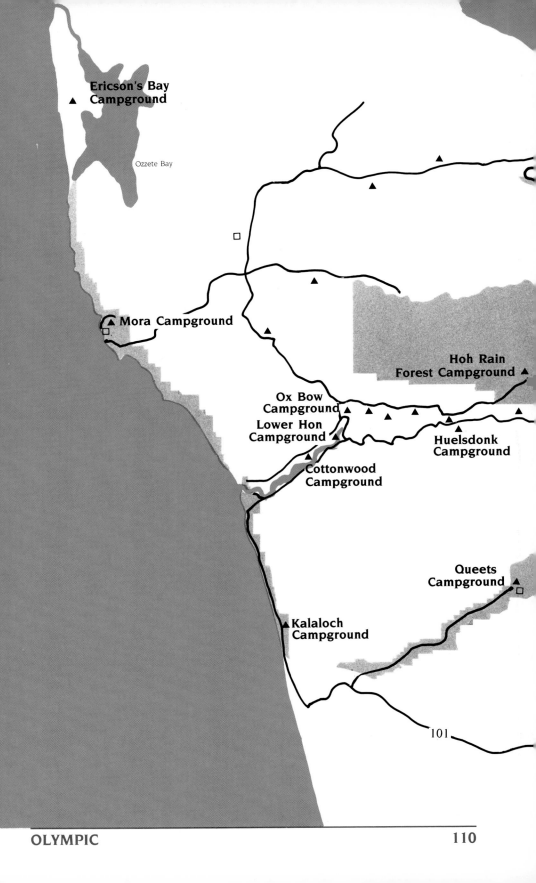

Ericson's Bay
Campground

Ozzete Bay

Mora Campground

Hoh Rain
Forest Campground

Ox Bow
Campground

Lower Hon
Campground

Huelsdonk
Campground

Cottonwood
Campground

Queets
Campground

Kalaloch
Campground

101

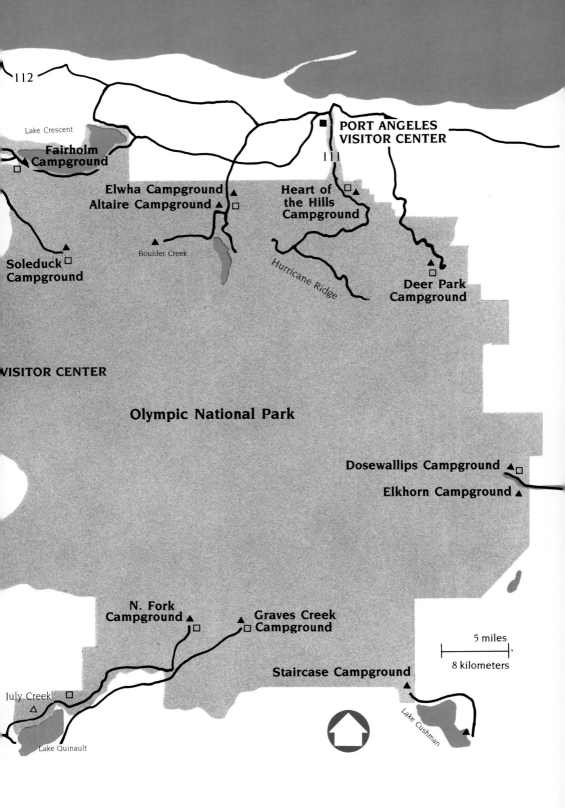

112

Lake Crescent

Fairholm Campground

PORT ANGELES VISITOR CENTER

111

Elwha Campground
Altaire Campground

Heart of the Hills Campground

Boulder Creek

Soleduck Campground

Hurricane Ridge

Deer Park Campground

VISITOR CENTER

Olympic National Park

Dosewallips Campground

Elkhorn Campground

N. Fork Campground

Graves Creek Campground

5 miles

8 kilometers

Staircase Campground

July Creek

Lake Cushman

Lake Quinault

Dosewallips * (elev. 1,640') is located 15 miles west of Brinnon on a partial dirt road. It has 33 sites for tents only and is open June through September.

Elwha (elev. 390') is located 10 miles west of Port Angeles in a heavily-wooded, level forest of hardwood trees across the road from the Elwha River. It has 41 sites and is open all year. Facilities include a ranger station and an amphitheater with evening interpretive programs.

Ericson's Bay * (elev. under 100') is located on the west shore of Ozette Lake and is accessible by boat only. It has 15 sites for tents only and is open all year. Swimming and boating are available.

Lake Crescent/Fairholm (elev. 580') is located 26 miles west of Port Angeles in a heavily wooded area on Lake Crescent. It has 87 sites and is open all year. Facilities include an amphitheater with evening interpretative programs and a dump station. The campground offers trailheads to nature hikes in the area. Adjacent facilities include a store, gas station, visitor center/ranger station and marina with swimming and boat launching facilities.

Graves Creek * (elev. 540') is located 20 miles east of Amanda Park on a dirt road. It has 45 sites and is closed when it snows.

Heart O' The Hills (elev. 1,807') is located 5.5 miles south of Port Angeles in a pretty fir forest. It has 105 sites and is open all year. Facilities include a ranger station, public telephones, and an amphitheater with evening interpretative programs. The campground offers trailheads to three hikes in the area. Loop A in the campground is accessible for handicapped.

Hoh (elev. 578') is located 22 miles southeast of Forks in a heavily-wooded, grassy area adjacent to the Hoh River in the Hoh Rain Forest. It has 95 sites, and is open all year. Facilities include a ranger station, an amphitheater with evening interpretive programs, a dump station, picnic sites and a visitor center. The campground offers trailheads to nature hikes in the area.

July Creek * (elev. 200') is located 6 miles northeast of Amanda Park on the shores of Quinault Lake in a beautiful stand of giant red cedar. It has 31 walk-in sites for tents only and is open all year. Boating and windsurfing are available on the lake, and a portion of the campground on the beach is for day use with tables and grills provided.

Kalaloch (elev. 100') is located 35 miles south of Forks in an open, level area on the ocean. It has 179 sites and is open all year. Facilities include a summer visitor center, a dump station, an amphitheater with evening interpretive programs and a store. Swimming is available. The campground is handicapped useable.

Mora (elev. sea level) is located 15 mi. W of Forks. It has 91 sites and is open all year. Facilities include a dump station and an amphitheater with evening interpretive programs. Swimming is available.

North Fork * (elev. 520') is located 20 mi. NE of Amanda Park. It has 8 sites for tents only and is open June through September.

Ozette * (sea level) is located 15 mi. SW of Sekiu. It has 14 sites and is open all year.

Queets * (elev. 290') is located 25 mi. SE of Queets. It has 26 sites for tents only and is open June through September.

Soleduck (elev. 1,680') is located 40 mi. SW of Port Angeles. It has 84 sites and is closed when it snows. Facilities include a dump station, an amphitheater with evening interpretive programs, and a store. Swimming is available. (Closed Oct. 86-May 88 due to road reconstruction).

Staircase (elev. 890') is located 19 mi. NW of Hoodsport. It has 63 sites, some suitable for small trailers, and is open all year. The campground has an amphitheater with evening interpretive programs.

LODGING

Kalaloch Lodge: On Hwy. 101 S on the beach 36 mi. S of Forks, WA; open all year; lodge rooms; motel; modern housekeeping cabins; dining room; coffee shop; cocktail lounge; store; service station; clam shovels to rent; reservations: Manager, Rt. 1, Box 1100, Forks, WA 98331, 206/962-2271

Lake Crescent Lodge: On Hwy. 101 21 mi. W of Port Angeles; open May-Oct.; lodge rooms; motel rooms; modern cottages; dining room; cocktail lounge; reservations: Manager, National Park Concessions, Inc., Star Rt. 1, Box 11, Port Angeles,WA 98362, 206/928-3211 (Note: Busses from Port Angeles pass daily on Hwy. 101.)

Log Cabin Resort: On NE end of Lake Crescent, 17 mi. W of Port Angeles on Hwy. 101 and 3 mi. on East Beach Road; open all year; motel units; cabins; restaurant; cocktail lounge; groceries; RV park; camping spaces; boat rentals & launching; fishing tackle; laundromat; reservations: Manager, 6540 East Beach Rd., Port Angeles, WA 98362, 206/928-3245

Sol Duc Hot Springs Resort: In the Soleduck River Valley, 40 mi. W of Port Angeles; open May-Oct., depending on snow conditions; cabins; motel units; kitchenettes; camping cabins; swimming pools; hot mineral baths; dining room; fountain service; store; fishing tackle; camping supplies; curios; gifts; reservations: Manager, P.O. Box 1355, Port Angeles, WA 98362, 206/327-3583.

There are over 600 miles of hiking trails in Olympic National Park. They vary from sea level to 7,965 feet in elevation. They can vary in duration from short walks to several weeks. However, they have one thing in common, and that is, they can be wet. Be prepared for rain.

The following publications are recommended:

A Climber's Guide to the Olympic Mountains (The Mountaineers)
Olympic Mountain Trail Guide by Robert L. Wood
Mountaineering—The Freedom of the Hills (The Mountaineers)
Roads and Trails of Olympic National Park by Fred Leissler
U.S.G.S. 15-min. Quadrangle Maps, Mt. Tom and Mt. Olympus
U.S.G.S. Topographical map, Olympic National Park and vicinity

In addition, the Park Service provides free hiking pamphlets organized by geographical area.

Listed below are a few recommended day hikes.

Heart O' The Hills & Hurricane Ridge

Lake Creek Trail: 4.0mi/6.4km round trip; allow 2 hours; trailhead: Loop E of Heart O' The Hills campground. This trail features the dense vegetation of lowland forest.

Hurricane Hill Trail: 1.5 mi/2.4km one way; trailhead: end of Hurricane Ridge Road. Mountain peak vistas and a view of Port Angeles and the Straits of Juan de Fuca are at the top of this trail. Wildflowers are abundant in summer. The first .5 mi. is suitable for wheelchairs with assistance.

Meadow Loop Trails: trailhead: near Hurricane Ridge Lodge. These gentle trails offer wildflowers, blacktailed deer, and a typical subalpine environment and are suitable for wheelchairs with assistance before continuing on to Mt. Angeles and Klahhane Ridge.

Elwha

Cascade Rock Trail: 2.0mi/3.2km one way; trailhead: Elwha campground.

Griff Creek Trail: 2.8mi/4.5km one way; trailhead: behind ranger station. The trail has some sections of steep switchbacks.

Krause Bottom Trail: 2.0mi/3.2km to river; trailhead: end of Whiskey Bend Road S of campground. This trail follows a wooded ridge above the Elwha River before descending .5 mi. down to the River. Trout fishing is available.

Lake Crescent

Marymere Falls: .75mi/1.2km one way. The trail leads through flowering plants and forest on its way to this spectacular 90' waterfall. The first .5 mi. is suitable for wheelchairs with assistance.

Mount Storm King Trail: 2.75mi/4.4km one way; trailhead: Marymere Falls Trail. This steep trail offers good views of Lake Crescent below.

Pyramid Peak Trail: 3.5mi/5.6km one way; ascent 2600'; trailhead: N shore of Lake. This trail offers good views of Lake Crescent from the WWII aircraft spotter station at its summit.

Spruce Railway Trail: 4.0mi/6.4km one way; trailheads: North Shore or Lyre River trailheads (trail connects the two). This relatively flat trail offers good views of Lake Crescent as it parallels the WWI Spruce Railway bed.

Soleduck

Soleduck Falls/Lover's Lane: 6.0mi/9.6km loop; trailhead: end of Soleduck River Road. Soleduck Falls trail leads 1 mi. through dense forest to the Falls, and Lover's Lane continues a 5-mi. loop to Sol Duc Resort.

Mink Lake Trail: 2.5mi/4.0km one way; ascent 1000'; trailhead: Sol Duc Resort. The trail climbs through dense forest to the lake, where trout fishing is available.

Lake Ozette to the Pacific Coast

Indian Village Trail: 3.3mi/5.3km one way; trailhead: end of Lake Ozette road. This northern trail provides a wooden walkway to the beach. A 3.0mi/4.8km walk south along the beach provides views of Indian petroglyphs, Ozette Island and Cape Alava, the western-most point in the contiguous U.S. The trail connects here with the Sand Point Trail for a 9.0mi/14.4km loop.

Sand Point Trail: 3.0mi/4.8km one way; trailhead: Lake Ozette road. This is the southern trail to the coast; see Indian Village Trail above.

Mora—Lapush

Third Beach Trail: 0.7mi/1.1km one way; trailhead: LaPush road, 12 mi. W of U.S. 101. This trail leads to a sandy beach.

Second Beach Trail: 0.6mi/1.0km one way; trailhead: LaPush road, 14 mi. W of U.S. 101. A sandy beach with tide pools and views of sea stacks is at the end of this trail.

Rialto Beach Trail: 0.1mi/0.2km one way. This paved trail to a beach overlook of James and Cake Islands is suitable for wheelchairs with assistance.

Hoh Rain Forest

Hall of Mosses Trail (0.75mi/1.2km round trip) and **Spruce Nature Trail** (1.75mi/2.8km round trip): trailhead: Visitor Center at end of Hoh road. Both trails offer good examples of the dense, lush vegetation of a rain forest and possibly a glimpse of deer or elk. There is a 0.5mi/0.8km paved mini-trail suitable for wheelchairs.

Kalaloch

Ruby Beach Trail and short beach trails: all .05mi/.08km to .15mi/.24km; trailhead: U.S. 101. These 7 trails lead to distinct beaches with some offering tidepools and others beachcombing and clamming (in season).

Queets

A 3.0mi/4.8km loop trail begins at Queets campground and goes to Queets and Sams River, where trout fishing is available.

Staircase

Shady Lane Nature Trail: 2.0mi/3.2km round trip; trailhead: across bridge from ranger station.

Staircase Rapids Trail: 0.5mi/0.8km one way to Rapids; trailhead: near ranger station. The trail ascends through heavy virgin forest along the Skokomish River to the Rapids and continues along Four Stream.

BRIEF HISTORY

Early Native Americans of the Olympic Peninsula were blessed with a moderate climate and an abundant food supply from both the land and sea. There were nine tribes who had a similar culture and lived more or less peacefully. Distinctive to their culture was the famous "Potlatch", where all differences were buried at least temporarily. Tribes traveled hundreds of miles for these festive occasions brought on by what brings us together today—birth, marriage and death.

Mt. Olympus was named by British Captain John Mearos on an expedition in 1788. The Olympic mountains, due to their remote location, were a long time in being explored. The first major expedition was led by Army Lt. Joseph O'Neil in 1885, who explored the northeast corner of the peninsula. He returned in 1890 to explore the southern Olympics.

In 1897 President Grover Cleveland created the Olympic Forest Reserve. However, it was reduced in size by subsequent presidents. In 1938 Congress passed a bill creating Olympic National Park, which was signed by President Franklin D. Roosevelt on June 29, 1938. In 1953 the Bogachiel Strip was added to the Park and in 1976 the Coastal Strip was also added.

AUTHOR'S COMMENTS

Olympic National Park is three parks in one. They are the coastal section along the Pacific Ocean, the unique rain forest areas of the Quinalt, Hoh and Queets Rivers, and the mountainous area dominated by Mt. Olympus (elev. 7965'). The Park, in addition to its wondrous beauty, has, in the author's opinion, the greatest number of activities available of any western park. This fact is not lost on the populace of very active oudoorsmen of the Pacific Northwest. The Park's visitation of approximately three million visitors annually speaks for itself.

Petrified Forest

LOCATION:	Eastern Arizona
ACCESS:	Travelers going east on I-40 exit at Holbrook on Hwy. 180 and enter the south entrance; travelers going west on I-40 exit at north entrance to the Park.
SEASON:	All year (Road open but facilities closed Christmas Day and New Year's Day)
HOURS:	Vary from 6 a.m.–7 p.m. in summer to 8 a.m.–5 p.m. in winter on Rocky Mountain Standard Time.
ENTRANCE FEES:	$5/vehicle/week; $2/person all others/week; $15 annual; $25 Golden Eagle
GAS & FOOD:	Snacks at Fred Harvey Fountain (south entrance); gas and restaurant at Painted Desert Visitor Center (north entrance)
NEAREST PROPANE:	North entrance to Park
CAMPGROUNDS:	None in Park; private campground under construction at time of writing directly outside south entrance to Park
LODGING:	None in Park
ADJACENT FACILITIES:	*Navajo* (14 mi. east of Park on I-40) Painted Desert Motel and Trailer Park: full hook-ups, showers, store, open all year
	Holbrook (15 mi. W of south entrance) KOA: full hook-ups, showers, propane, store, open all year; OK-RV Park: full hook-ups, showers, adjacent to shopping center, open all year.
VISITOR CENTER:	Painted Desert Visitor Center (north entrance)
MUSEUM:	Rainbow Forest Museum (south entrance) with samples and exhibits showing, among other things, how the petrified wood was formed.
PICNICKING:	Only at Rainbow Forest area and Chinde Point (overlooking Painted Desert)
GIFT SHOPS:	Rainbow Forest Curios and at Painted Desert
ACTIVITIES:	Walking; hiking; photography; wilderness backpacking and camping (permit required); various park-sponsored activities (posted at Visitor Center)
CLIMATE:	Warm days and cool nights in summer; cool days and cold nights in winter; less than 10 inches of precipitation, with 40% the result of summer thunderstorms
ELEVATION:	5,300 to 6,235 ft.
SIZE:	147 sq. miles
ANNUAL VISITATION:	Approximately three-quarters million
PETS:	Must be on leash; not permitted in wilderness areas or in public buildings

FACILITIES
FOR DISABLED: Restrooms at Rainbow Forest Museum, Painted Desert Visitor Center, Puerco Ruin (summer only) and Painted Desert Inn; film and information in large script at Painted Desert Visitor Center

INFORMATION: *Supt. Petrified Forest National Park*
Petrified Forest National Park, AZ 86028
602/524-6228

HIKING

Interpretive Trails

Giant Logs Trail: .5mi/.8km loop; allow 30 minutes. The trailhead is behind the Rainbow Forest Museum, which is two miles from the southern Park boundary. The area contains some of the largest petrified logs in the Park.

Long Logs Trail: .5mi/.8km loop; allow 30 minutes. Here is the largest concentration of petrified wood in the Park. Just off the Long Logs Trail is a short hike to Agate House, a partially restored pueblo last inhabited by Indians some 700 years ago.

Crystal Forest Trail: .8mi/1.3km; allow 30 minutes. This area had a dense concentration of petrified wood which was heavily destroyed by souvenir hunters and gem collectors and which then prompted citizens to petition Congress for federal protection.

Blue Mesa Trail: .8mi/1.3km one way; allow 45 minutes round trip. The trail descends steeply into the badlands. Colorful scenery abounds along the way.

WILDERNESS HIKING

Backpack hiking and overnight camping are allowed in the two wilderness areas of the Park. Painted Desert in the north consists of 43,020 acres, with parking and the trailhead at Kachina Point. Rainbow Forest in the south consists of 7,240 acres, with parking and the trailhead at Flattops. A permit is required, at no charge, and can be obtained at the Museum or Visitor Center on a first-come basis. Topographical maps are recommended for wilderness hiking and can be purchased at the Visitor Center or Museum.

BRIEF HISTORY

Early Spanish explorers found no evidence of Indian habitation in their exploration of the southwest in 1540. However, Indians had lived here as early as approximately 6000 B.C. The Anasazi, a highly developed Indian people, were prominent and then mysteriously disappeared around A.D. 1400.

The Park area was virtually untouched by white men until the mid 1850's. Then, by various expedition accounts, word of mouth, and newspaper stories, the word spread. The completion of the Atlantic and Pacific railroads in 1883 brought in settlers and tourists in greatly increasing numbers.

The 1890's saw the exploration end and the exploitation begin to such a

---

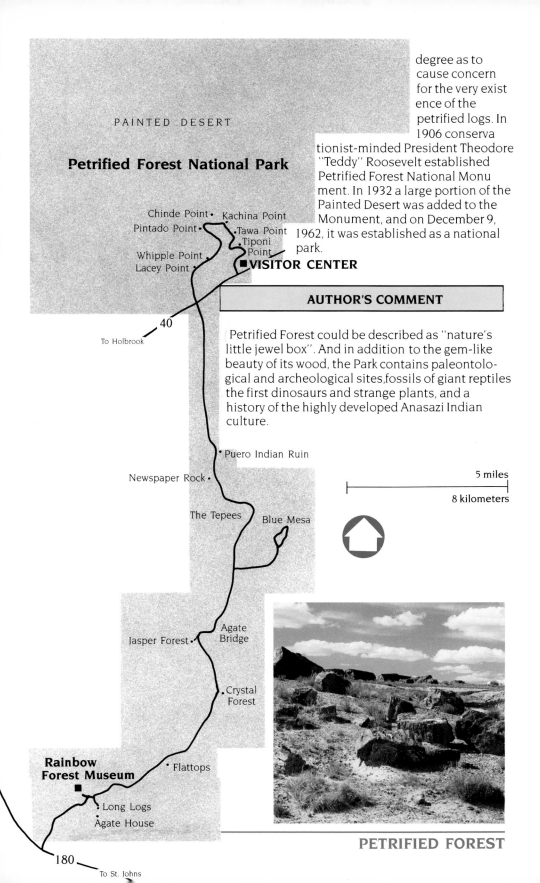

PAINTED DESERT

Petrified Forest National Park

Chinde Point • Kachina Point •
Pintado Point • • Tawa Point
                  • Tiponi
Whipple Point •   Point
Lacey Point •   ■ VISITOR CENTER

40
To Holbrook

• Puero Indian Ruin

Newspaper Rock •

The Tepees •   Blue Mesa

Agate
Bridge
Jasper Forest •

• Crystal
  Forest

Rainbow
Forest Museum   • Flattops
■

• Long Logs
Agate House

180
To St. Johns

degree as to cause concern for the very exist ence of the petrified logs. In 1906 conserva tionist-minded President Theodore "Teddy" Roosevelt established Petrified Forest National Monu ment. In 1932 a large portion of the Painted Desert was added to the Monument, and on December 9, 1962, it was established as a national park.

| AUTHOR'S COMMENT |

Petrified Forest could be described as "nature's little jewel box". And in addition to the gem-like beauty of its wood, the Park contains paleontolo- gical and archeological sites, fossils of giant reptiles the first dinosaurs and strange plants, and a history of the highly developed Anasazi Indian culture.

5 miles
8 kilometers

PETRIFIED FOREST

Redwood

LOCATION:	North coast of California
ACCESS:	U.S. 101 runs north and south through the Park
SEASON:	All year
HOURS:	24 hours/day
ENTRANCE FEE:	None
GAS, FOOD & LODGING:	In Crescent City, Orick, Klamath
NEAREST PROPANE:	Along Hwy. 101
CAMPGROUNDS:	Most camping is in 3 state parks in the Park; reservations advised; no hook-ups; showers; some primitive camping
ADJACENT FACILITIES:	Numerous motels, restaurants, stores and RV parks all along U.S. 101; Forest Service campgrounds off Hwy. 199 east of Gasquet; Patrick's Point State Park, 5 mi. N of Trinidad, with a total of 123 sites with facilities and reservations similar to other State Parks.
VISITOR CENTERS:	Redwood Information Center; Park Headquarters at Crescent City; Hiouchi Ranger Station and the Prairie Creek State Park Visitor Center offer programs and exhibits
PICNICKING:	Throughout Park at designated spots
TOURS:	Shuttle-bus tour from Redwood Information Center— summer only (nominal fees)
ACTIVITIES:	Hiking; canoeing; float and kayak trips on the Smith River; swimming; fishing (license required); guided tide pool walks; elk watching; interpretive programs
CLIMATE:	Damp, cool summers along coast; warm and dry inland; mild, wet winters
ELEVATION:	Near sea level
SIZE:	166 sq. miles
ANNUAL VISITATION:	Approximately one-half million
PETS:	Must be on leash; not allowed on trails or in backcountry; must have current license or proof of rabies to enter State Park; nominal entrance and camping fee
FACILITIES FOR DISABLED:	At Hiouchi, Crescent City, Klamath and Orick areas
INFORMATION:	*Supt. Redwood National Park* *1111 Second Street* *Crescent City, CA 95531* 707/464-6101 *Redwood Information Center (south entrance):* 707/488-3461

• Campgrounds have tables, grills, modern comfort stations, hot water and showers (Gold Bluff Beach has cold water only).
• Fees are $2 for day use, $6 for overnight stay and $1 for bicyclers and hikers.
• Limit of stay is 15 days in summer, 30 days Oct.–May.
• Gathering of dead and down firewood is permitted.
• Reservations for state park campgrounds are advised during summer months and may be made up to 8 weeks in advance or as late as 2 days prior to arrival: Mistix, P.O. Box 85705, San Diego, CA 92138/5705; 800/446-7275.

Jedediah Smith Redwoods S.P. is located 9 mi. E of Crescent City on Hwy. 199 in a densely-wooded, "old growth" redwood grove. It has 109 sites, with some located adjacent to the Smith River allowing more light, and is open all year. The campground has some sites which can accommodate trailers up to 30 ft. and campers up to 31 ft. Facilities include a picnic area on the Smith River, visitor center, a campfire area with programs in summer months, and a dump station. The Park serves as a trailhead for numerous hikes including a nature trail.

Del Norte Coast Redwoods S.P. (Mill Creek) is located 7 mi. S of Crescent City on Hwy. 101 and 2½ mi. on Park road in a dense forest of redwood trees. It has 145 sites and is open from April to October. The campground has some sites to accommodate trailers up to 30 ft. and campers up to 31 ft. It has a dump station and serves as a trailhead for Trestle Loop Trail.

Prairie Creek Redwoods S.P. is located 5 mi. N of Orick in a thick grove of redwoods. It has 75 sites with some on the edge of the grove, allowing more light, and is open all year. The campground has sites for 24 ft. trailers and 27 ft. campers. It has a picnic area on Elk Prairie.

*NOTE: There is an environmental campground with 6 sites off the Davison Road to Gold Bluff's Beach. Advance reservations are required (Prairie Creek State Park Headquarters). The fee is $6/night and limit of stay is 7 days.

Gold Bluffs Beach is located off Davidson Road, an unpaved road intersecting U.S. 101 3.6 mi. S of Prairie Creek Park Headquarters. It is approximately 6 miles from the intersection and consists of 25 sites situated on the beach. The campground is open all year but wet weather sometimes makes area inaccessible. It is on a first-come basis.

Walk-In Campgrounds

Nickel Creek is a 20-minute walk from the end of Enders Beach Road off U.S. 101 just south of Crescent City. It consists of 6 sites. Facilities include tables, fire rings and compost toilets. Water is available but must be boiled.

DeMartin is a 45-minutes walk off U.S. 101 about 2 mi. N of Lagoon Cr. It consists of 10 sites overlooking the Pacific Ocean. Facilities include compost toilets and potable water. No open fires are allowed.

Flint Ridge is a 10-minutes walk off Coastal Drive approximately 2 mi. off U.S. 101. It consists of 10 sites overlooking the Pacific Ocean. Facilities include compost toilets and potable water. No open fires are allowed.

To Oregon
199

101 **Hiouchi Area**
Park Headquarters / State Park
Cresent City Area

Mill Creek ▲

Nickel Creek △

DeMartin △

Klamath Area

Flint Ridge △

Prairie Creek Area ▲■
▲
Gold Bluffs Beach
Lady Bird Johnson Grove
Orick Area

Redwood Information Center ■

101

Redwood National Park

5 miles
8 kilometers

There are over 60 trails, including several nature trails, within the boundaries of Redwood National Park. In addition, you may easily walk along the streams after they recede from winter's rain. The trails are detailed in the Redwood Natural History Association pamphlet "Trails" which is for sale for a nominal fee. Listed below are some of the most popular.

Jedediah Smith Area

Simpson-Reed Grove: 0.6mi/0.9km loop; easy; trailhead: Hwy. 190 turn-out near Walker Rd. (milepost 3.0). This trail leads through an old-growth redwood forest with small streams, lush undergrowth, and giant fallen redwoods. A side trail through Peterson Grove returns to the loop.

Stout Grove: 0.5mi/0.8km loop; easy; trailhead: Howland Hill Rd. parking area. This area contains the Park's largest redwood in volume at 16' diameter and 340' height. There are restrooms, and the hike is suitable for handicapped.

Nickerson Ranch-Mill Creek Trail: 2.0mi/3.2km loop; moderate; trailhead: Howland Hill Rd. 2.1mi. from west end of pavement (3.4 mi. from east). This trail offers a hollow tree to walk into, a stream beneath a fallen redwood, and several forest habitats boasting a rich variety of life.

Boy Scout Tree Trail: 7.4mi/11.8km round trip; strenuous; trailhead: Howland Hill Rd. 2.3 mi. from west end of pavement (3.2 mi. from east). This trail through mature redwood forest comes to a fork in 3 miles; the right fork leads to the Boy Scout Tree and the left leads to Fern Falls.

Del Norte Coast Area

Endert's Beach Trail: 1.2mi/1.9km round trip; moderate; trailhead: 4 mi. S of Crescent City at end of Endert's Beach Road. This trail views the ocean below on its descent to Endert's Beach.

Coastal Trail/Last Chance Section: 6.0mi/9.6km one-way; strenuous; trailhead: near milepost 15.6 on Hwy. 101 S of Crescent City. This trail follows an old highway route through majestic redwoods, crosses the Damnation Creek Trail, and follows a steep grade to Nickel Creek and the Endert's Beach trailhead.

Damnation Creek Trail: 5.0mi/8.0km round trip; strenuous; trailhead: Hwy. 101 milepost 16.0 south of Crescent City. This trail leads through majestic old

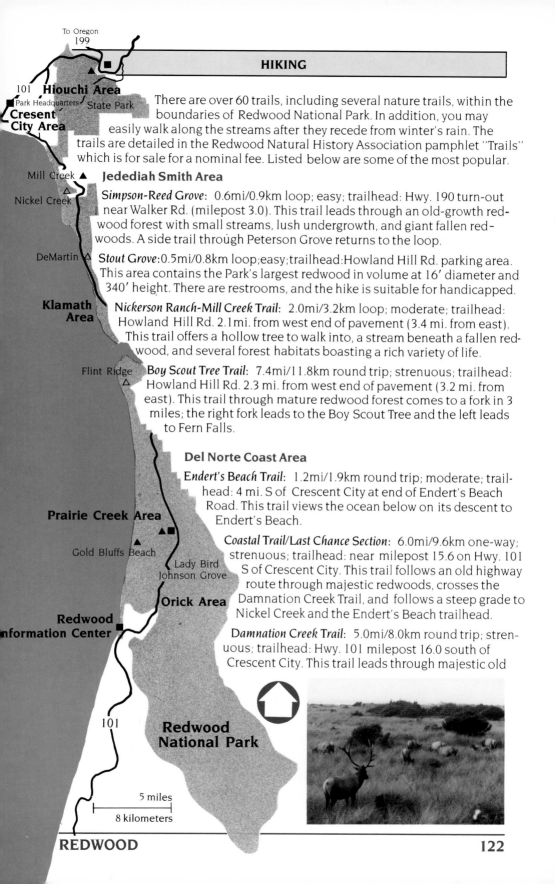

growth forest and past huge rhododendrons and small streams on its 1000 ft. descent to a sheltered cove with an abundance of sea mammals.

Klamath Area

Coastal Trail/DeMartin Section: 5.0mi/8.0km one way; strenuous; trailheads: N end of Wilson Creek Bridge and milepost 15.6. This trail affords views of the Pacific Ocean and passes through logged areas, abandoned farm sites, and old-growth redwoods.

Yurok Loop Trail: 1.0mi/1.6km loop; moderate; trailhead: N end of Lagoon Creek picnic area. The trail offers views of the Pacific along with views of wildflowers and sea mammals on its climb up the coastal bluff. A self-guiding brochure at the trailhead describes the local Native American culture. Restrooms are available.

Coastal Trail/Hidden Beach Section: 4.0mi/6.4km one way; moderate; trailhead: Klamath Overlook. This trail follows the coastal bluff through grassland and forest areas and offers good chances to view whales, birdlife and coastal wildflowers.

Flint Ridge Trail: 9.0mi/14.4km round trip; strenuous; trailhead: Klamath Beach Road. This trail follows the shoreline of Marshall Pond before ascending into old-growth redwood forest.

Prairie Creek Area

Fern Canyon: 0.7mi/1.1km loop; easy; trailhead: Davison Rd., 7 mi. from Hwy. 101. Luxuriant ferns cover the walls of this canyon. The trail follows Home Creek up to the site of an historic mining settlement.

Miners Ridge-James Irvine Trail: 10.2mi/16.3km loop; moderate; trailhead: Prairie Creek Visitor Center. These trails provide exploration of old-growth redwood trees, wildlife, and a visit to Fern Canyon.

Big Tree Wayside (50 yds. to "Big Tree"): trailhead: 1 mi. N of Prairie Creek Visitor Center. This trail leads to the Big Tree (304' tall) and provides access to a variety of beautiful trails. Restrooms are available.

Cathedral Trees-Rhododendron Trail Loop: 6.5mi/10.4km loop; strenuous; trailhead: the "Big Tree". The trail climbs 800 ft. and then descends through majestic redwood.

Orick Area

Forest Renewal Trail: 1.5mi/2.4km round trip; moderate; trailhead: 3 mi. N of Orick on Hwy. 101, then W 2 mi. on Davison Road. This trail offers views of the early stages of redwood forest regeneration after the area was logged in the 1960's.

Lost Man Creek Trail: 1.5mi/2.4km round trip; easy; trailhead: 3.5 mi. N of Orick on Hwy. 101, then 1 mi. E. This trail leads past the World Heritage dedication site to a cascade on Lost Man Creek.

Lady Bird Johnson Grove: 1.0mi/1.6km loop; easy; trailhead: 2.5 mi. E on Bald Hills Rd. from Hwy. 101. This trail leads through mature redwood forest to the 1968 National Park dedication site. Self-guiding brochure at trailhead. Restrooms are available.

Redwood Creek Trail: 1.5mi/2.4km to summer-only bridge; 8.0mi/12.8km to Tall Trees Grove in summer, one way; moderate; trailhead: from Hwy. 101, 0.3 mi. E on Bald Hills Road and turn right. (Shuttlebus available in summer). The trail follows Redwood Creek to Tall Trees Grove. Restrooms are available.

Tall Trees–Emerald Ridge Loop: 4.0mi/6.4km loop; summer only; strenuous; take shuttlebus to trailhead; allow 4-5 hours including shuttle. The Tall Trees Trail descends 800 ft. into the grove with the world's tallest known tree (367.8 ft.) and then follows Redwood Creek upstream to return to trailhead via Emerald Ridge Trail. Restrooms are available. Camping is allowed upstream from the first creek junction, except for areas .25 mile on either side of the Tall Trees Grove. Permits are required and can be obtained at the trailhead or Redwood Information Center.

HISTORY

The earliest inhabitants of the Redwood National Park area were the Indian tribes of the Chiula, Tolowa, and Yurok. They lived mainly around the stream banks, and salmon was their main dish. Early Spanish explorers were the first white men to visit the area, and in 1828 Jedediah Smith, a fur trapper, explored the general area including the Smith River. A gold strike in 1850 at Gold Bluffs Beach started the first invasion of pioneers.

Logging was initiated at this time, and the desirability of redwood lumber was first acclaimed. The wood was rot- and insect-resistant in addition to having a natural beauty. At first the very size of the trees limited the loggers, but as time went on, methods were developed and the trees came under heavy harvest.

Conservation groups, mainly The Save-the-Redwoods League, were instrumental in establishing the three state parks which are within the national park boundaries. In 1968 Redwood National Park was established to protect the remaining "old-growth groves". However, the watershed affecting the original acreage was severely affected by intensive logging in the adjacent forest. Efforts by the Sierra Club combined with publications from the National Geographic Society stimulated Congress to enlarge the original acreage by an additional 48,000 acres in 1978.

Congress also authorized 33 million dollars for a ten- to fifteen-year land rehabilitation project to stabilize the badly damaged watershed. There has never been a project of this magnitude, and the Park Service had to proceed "without the book". It has been a step-by-step process. The first goal was to stop erosion and the second to reestablish the natural vegetation. The project has had impressive results, which are evident in the Park today.

AUTHOR'S COMMENT

There's a famous quotation attributed to President Reagan stating, "If you've seen one redwood, you've seen them all." But to see them all in a grove—you've seen something you won't forget.

REDWOOD

Rocky Mountain

LOCATION: North central Colorado

ACCESS: Through Grand Lake on Hwy. 34 from the west; through Estes Park on Highways 34, 36, and 7 from the east

SEASON: All year (Trail Ridge Road closed in winter)

HOURS: 24 hours/day

ENTRANCE FEES: $5/vehicle/week; $2/person all others/week; $15 annual; $25 Golden Eagle

GAS & FOOD: Grand Lake and Estes Park; snacks on top of Trail Ridge Road in the Park (summer only)

NEAREST PROPANE: Grand Lake and Estes Park

LODGING: None in Park

CAMPGROUNDS: Moraine Park and Glacier Basin require reservations in summer; other campgrounds on first-come basis; tents only at Longs Peak; no hookups or showers

ADJACENT FACILITIES: See below

VISITOR CENTERS: Park Headquarters; Moraine Park; Alpine; Kawuneeche (West Unit)

MUSEUM: At Moraine Park

PICNICKING: Along major roads throughout the Park

GIFT SHOP: Fall River Store adjacent to Alpine Visitor Center on Trail Ridge Road

TOURS: Ranger-conducted hikes in summer (daily program at Park Headquarters and visitor centers)

FISHING: Colorado fishing license required; artificial lures only for adults; prohibited at Bear Lake

ACTIVITIES: Hiking; horseback riding; backpacking; cross-country and alpine skiing in winter; interpretive programs

CLIMATE: Cool, pleasant summers with afternoon thundershowers common; snow in winter

ELEVATION: 7,620 to 14,255 ft.

SIZE: 413 sq. miles

ANNUAL VISITATION: Approximately three million

PETS: Prohibited on trails, in backcountry and in public buildings; permitted on leash on roads and in camping and picnic areas

FACILITIES FOR DISABLED: Handicamp in backcountry; accessible visitor centers; 2 paved trails; scenic drives; captioned programs; braille literature

INFORMATION: *Supt. Rocky Mountain National Park*
Estes Park, CO 80517
303/586-2371 (east side)
303/627-3471 (west side)
Park Emergency: 586-2371 (Mon-Thurs 6 AM-1 AM; Fri-Sun
6 AM-2 AM)—other: 911

CAMPGROUNDS

• All campgrounds (except backcountry) have tables, grills and modern comfort stations (pit toilets in winter).
• Wood gathering is prohibited except when authorized at backcountry campsites; wood is available for sale.
• Campgrounds have no hook-ups or showers.
• There are dump stations at Moraine Park, Glacier Basin and Timber Creek.
• The campground fee is $6 per night except backcountry campgrounds, which are free.
• Campgrounds fill early in the day during summer.
• Group camping reservations: Rocky Mountain Nat'l Park, Backcountry Office, Estes Park, CO 80517-8397; 303/586-4459.
• Camping is limited to 7 days parkwide June-September.

Glacier Basin (elev. 8500') is located 9 mi. W of Estes Park on Bear Lake Road in a level, forested area adjacent to a mountain meadow. The campground has 152 individual sites and 12 group sites and is open June-Oct. Facilities include public telephones and a campfire amphitheater. This campground is on a reservation system (see below). Fishing is available. Interdenominational church services are held at the campground on Sundays. Maximum trailer length is 27'; motorhome is 30'.

Moraine Park (elev. 8200') is located 3 mi. W of Headquarters Visitor Center on Bear Lake Road in a level, forested area adjacent to a mountain meadow. The campground has 250 sites; two loops in the campground are open all year. Facilities include telephones and a campfire amphitheater. Fishing is available. This campground is on a reservation system (see below). Maximum trailer length is 27'; motorhome is 30'.

> *Reservations for Glacier Basin and Moraine Park:* Reservations may be made at Park Headquarters *in person* (no phone reservations) or through Ticketron (P.O. Box 2715 San Francisco, CA 94126-2715). Camping fee is $8 per night during reservation period.

Longs Peak (elev. 9500') is located 11 mi. S of Estes Park and 1 mi. W off CO. 7. *This is a tents-only campground* with 30 sites and is open year round but water is turned off after Labor Day. There are comfort stations with handicapped access. Campsites are on a first-come basis with a limit of 3 days in summer.

Aspenglen (elev. 8230') is located 5 mi. W of Estes Park near the Fall River Entrance. It has 26 sites all suitable for tents or small trailers including some walk-in sites, and it is open June through September. Facilities include telephones and a campfire amphitheater. Campground sites are on a first-come basis.

Timber Creek (elev. 8900') is located 10 mi. N of Grand Lake on Trail Ridge Road in a fairly level, forested area. It has 100 sites, all suitable for tents and small trailers, and a few sites for larger vehicles. The campground is open all year. Facilities include telephones, a campfire amphitheater and a dump station.

Campground sites are on a first-come basis. Fishing is available. This is the only campground in the Park west of the Continental Divide (except backcountry).

Backcountry Camping

A permit is required for all overnight stays. Reservation requests by mail or in person are accepted year round. No phone requests June through September. Permits are available at Park Headquarters, the Kawuneeche Visitor Center (West Unit), and some ranger stations. There are 239 sites, 41 of which allow wood fires; the rest allow stoves. Each campsite has a 3-day limit. Melt-out dates vary from mid-May to mid-July. Backcountry Office telephone: 303/586-4459 or 303/586-2371.

ADJACENT FACILITIES

In ESTES PARK:

Lodging: Chamber of Commerce, Estes Park, CO 80517
1-800-654-0949 in Colorado, 1-800-621-5888 in other states

Campgrounds: (all in Estes Park, CO 80517)

Estes Park CG: 5 mi. SW on CO 66 off US 36; open 6/1-9/1; reservations: Box 3517; 303/586-4188

KOA Estes Park: 1.5 mi. E on US 34; open 5/15-9/15; full hook-ups; flush toilets; showers; sanitary dump station; store; reservations: Davis Gulch Rt.; 303/586-2888

Manor RV *Park &* Motel: 1¼ mi. S on Riverside Dr.; open all year; full hook-ups; flush toilets; showers; sanitary dump station; propane; near store; reservations: 1701 E. Riverside Dr.; 303/586-3251

Mary's Lake CG: 2.5 mi. S on Hwy. 7, 1.5 mi. W on Peakview Dr.; open 5/15-9/15; full hook-ups; flush toilets; showers; sanitary dump station; propane; store; reservations: Box 2514; 303/586-4411

National Park Resort: W on US 34 at Fall River entrance to Park; open 5/1-9/31; full hook-ups; flush toilets; showers; sanitary dump station; near store; reservations: Moraine Rt.; 303/586-4563

Paradise Trailer Park: 2 mi. SW on US 36, ½ mi. W on Hwy. 66; open all year; full hook-ups; flush toilets; showers; sanitary dump station; store; reservations: Moraine Rt.; 303/586-5513

Spruce Lake RV *Park:* 1 mi. W on US 36, ¼ mi. S on Mary's Lake Rd.; open all year; full hook-ups; flush toilets; showers; sanitary dump station; propane; store; reservations: Box 3381; 303/586-2889

In GRAND LAKE:

Lodging: Chamber of Commerce, Grand Lake, CO 80447; 303/627-3402 or (in state) 800/826-8869

Campgrounds:
Winding River RV CG: 1 mi. N on US 34, 1½ mi. W on paved and gravel road; open Memorial Day–10/1; full hook-ups; flush toilets; showers; sanitary dump station; store; reservations: Box 629, Grand Lake, CO 80447; 303/466-1939

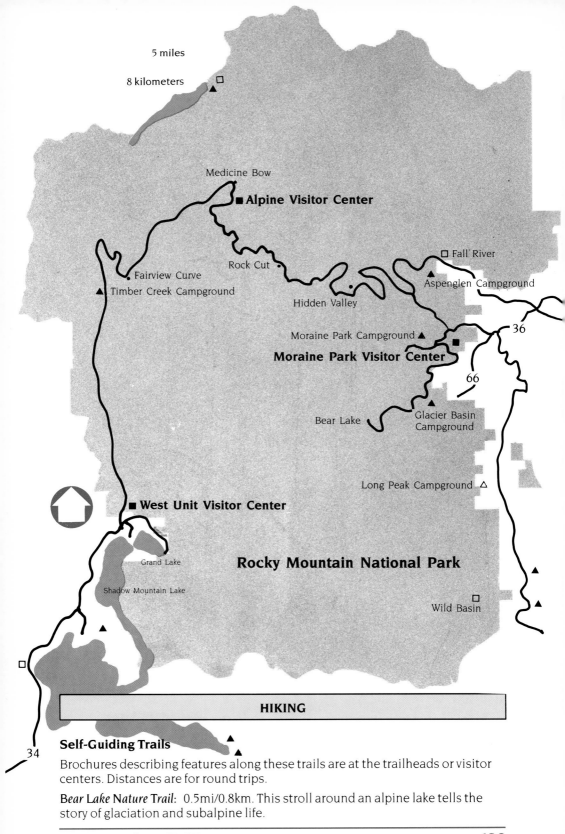

5 miles

8 kilometers

Medicine Bow

■ **Alpine Visitor Center**

Rock Cut

□ Fall River

Aspenglen Campground

• Fairview Curve
▲ Timber Creek Campground

Hidden Valley

Moraine Park Campground ▲

Moraine Park Visitor Center

36

66

Bear Lake

Glacier Basin
Campground

Long Peak Campground △

■ **West Unit Visitor Center**

Grand Lake

Rocky Mountain National Park

Shadow Mountain Lake

□
Wild Basin

| **HIKING** |

34

Self-Guiding Trails

Brochures describing features along these trails are at the trailheads or visitor centers. Distances are for round trips.

Bear Lake Nature Trail: 0.5mi/0.8km. This stroll around an alpine lake tells the story of glaciation and subalpine life.

Never Summer Ranch: 1.0mi/1.6km. The landscape and cabins tell the story of homesteading and dude ranch life in the central Rockies during the early 20th century.

Longs Peak Trail: 16.0mi/26.0km. The main hiking trail to the park's highest peak leads through subalpine forests, tundra, and glacial landscapes. Technical equipment sometimes required.

Lulu City: 7.2mi/11.6km. Traces of log cabins are all that remain of a once-booming mining town.

Moraine Park Nature Trail: .25mi/.4km. This easy stroll helps you identify local plants and animals.

Sprague Lake Trail: 0.5mi/0.8km. Ideal for wheelchair visitors, this is a level walk on which to use all your senses.

Tundra World: Short trails lead from both the Forest Canyon and Rock Cut Overlooks.

Rocky Mountain National Park has some 355 miles of trails. They can be divided into a number of geographic areas: Mummy Range, Moraine Park, Bear Lake Road, Bear Lake Trailhead, Longs Peak, East Edge Summits, Wild Basin, Trail Ridge Road, Colorado River, and Grand Lake. For more detailed information, see *Rocky Mountain National Park Hiking Trails* by Kent and Donna Dannen.

The most popular hiking area is that of Bear Lake. The following summarizes a number of trails by degree of difficulty:

Mileages are one-way. Level of Use: H = High; M = Moderate; L = Low.

Easy Trails:

From Sprague Lake Picnic Area: Sprague Lake Nature Trail—½ mile around the lake. (M)

From Glacier Gorge Parking Area: Alberta Falls—0.6 mile, 160 ft. elevation gain. (H)

From Bear Lake Parking Area: Bear Lake Nature Trail—½ mile around the lake. (A nature trail guide for this trail is available at visitor centers and Bear Lake). (H)
Nymph Lake—½ mile, 225 ft. elevation gain. (H)
Dream Lake—1.1 miles, 425 ft. elevation gain. (H)
Bierstadt Lake—1.6 miles, 255 ft. elevation gain. (M)

From Fern Lake Trailhead: The Pool—1.7 miles, 245 ft. elevation gain. (M)

From Wild Basin Ranger Station: Calypso Cascades—1.8 miles, 700 ft. elevation gain. (H)

From Longs Peak Ranger Station: Eugenia Mine—1.4 miles, 508 ft. elevation gain.(M)

From East Inlet Trailhead (Grand Lake): Adams Falls—0.3 mile, 79 ft. elevation gain. (M)

Moderate Trails:

From Bierstadt Lake Trailhead: Bierstadt Lake—1.4 miles, 566 ft. elevation gain. (When the Bear Lake Shuttle is in operation, you can ride the shuttle bus to Bear Lake, hike to Bierstadt Lake from there, and return via the Bierstadt Lake trail).(L)

From Glacier Gorge Parking Area: Lake Haiyaha—3.5 miles, 980 ft. elevation gain (difficult to hard). (L)
The Loch—2.7 miles, 940 ft. elevation gain. (H)
Mills Lake—2.5 miles, 700 ft. elevation gain. (H)

From Bear Lake Parking Area: Emerald Lake—1.8 miles, 605 ft. elevation gain. (M)
Lake Haiyaha—2.1 miles, 745 ft. elevation gain. (M)
Odessa Lake—4.1 miles, 1,215 ft. elevation gain, then 560 elevation loss from

Lake Helene. (H)
Fern Lake Trailhead via Odessa Lake and the Pool—8.5 miles, 1,865 ft. elevation loss from Odessa Lake. (H)

From Fern Lake Trailhead: Fern Lake—3.8 miles, 1,375 ft. elevation gain. (M)

From Cub Lake Trailhead: Cub Lake—2.3 miles, 540 ft. elevation gain; to Pool— 1.0 miles; return to trailhead—1.7 miles. (H)

From Twin Owls Trailhead or Gem Lake Trailhead: Gem Lake—1.8 miles, 910 ft. elevation gain (Twin Owls Trailhead); 2 miles, 1,090 ft. elevation gain (Gem Lake Trailhead). (M)

From Wild Basin Ranger Station: Ouzel Falls—2.7 miles, 950 ft. elevation gain. (H)

From Deer Ridge Junction: Deer Mountain—3 miles, 1,083 ft. elevation gain. (M)

From Colorado River Trailhead: Lulu City (Site)—3.1 miles, 300 ft. elevation gain.(M)

From North Inlet Trailhead: Cascade Falls—3.5 miles, 300 ft. elevation gain. (M)

More Difficult Trails:

From Glacier Gorge Parking Area: Black Lake—4.7 miles, 1,380 ft. elevation gain.(M)
Andrews Glacier—5 miles, 2,460 ft. elevation gain.
Timberline Falls—4.0 miles, 1,210 ft. elevation gain (to get to Sky Pond). (M)
Sky Pond—4.6 miles, 1,660 ft. elevation gain. (M)

From Bear Lake Parking Area: Flattop Mountain—4.4 miles, 2,849 ft. elevation gain. (H)

From Chapin Creek Trailhead: Ypsilon Mt., 3.5 miles, 2,874 ft. elevation gain. (L)

From Lawn Lake Trailhead: Lawn Lake—6.2 miles, 2,249 ft. elevation gain. (M)
Lake Ypsilon—4.5 miles, 2,180 ft. elevation gain. (L)

From Twin Sisters Trailhead: Twin Sisters Peaks—3.7 miles, 2,338 ft. elevation gain.(M)

From Longs Peak Ranger Station: Chasm Lake—4.2 miles, 2,360 ft. elevation gain.(H)
Longs Peak—8 miles, 4,855 ft. elevation gain. (H)

From Copeland Lake: Sandbeach Lake—4.2 miles, 1,971 ft. elevation gain. (M)

From Wild Basin Ranger Station: Ouzel Lake—4.9 miles, 1,510 ft. elevation gain. (L)
Bluebird Lake—6 miles, 2,478 ft. elevation gain. (L)
Finch Lake—4.5 miles, 1,442 ft. elevation gain (from Finch Lake TH). 5.3 miles, 1,412 ft. elevation gain (from Wild Basin RS) (L)
Thunder Lake—6.8 miles, 2,074 ft. elevation gain. (M)
Lion Lake No. 1—7 miles, 2,565 ft. elevation gain. (L)
Lion Lake No. 2—7.5 miles, 2,900 ft. elevation gain. (L)
Snowbank Lake—8.0 miles, 3,021 ft. elevation gain. (L)

From Timber Lake Trailhead: Timber Lake—4.8 miles, 2,060 ft. elevation gain. (M)

From North Inlet Trailhead: Lake Nanita—11 miles, 2,240 ft. elevation gain. (L)

From East Inlet Trailhead: Lake Verna—6.9 miles, 1,809 ft. elevation gain. (M)

BRIEF HISTORY

The land which is now Rocky Mountain National Park was used by Indians as early as 15,000 years ago. The introduction of horses by the Spanish changed the Plains Indian culture from that of farmers to that of nomadic hunters, with the tundra providing excellent summer hunting for thousands of years. By 1800 the Cheyenne, Arapaho, Utes and Shoshones occupied parts of the Park. Their ancient trails over the Continental Divide are still in evidence.

French and Spanish trappers were the first white explorers of the area. In 1820 an expedition led by Major Stephen Long, which was exploring the Louisiana Purchase territory, sighted the mountain which was to be named for their leader—Longs Peak. It is the highest peak in Colorado at elevation 14,255 feet.

Estes Park is named after Joel Estes and his son Milton, who were the first settlers, building a house and raising cattle in 1860. The late 1800's brought the start of tourism to Estes Park, and 1910 brought world recognition with the completion of the Stanley Hotel. This hotel was built by E. O. Stanley, the inventor of the Stanley Steamer automobile. The hotel is still doing business today, and a Stanley Steamer is on display in the lobby.

On the west side of the Park, Grand Lake was first a mining center in the 1880's. Then tourism got its start when, in 1907, "Squeaky" Bob Wheeler opened a tourist camp. And Grand Lake was on its way.

When you talk about the establishment of Rocky Mountain National Park, you are talking about Enos Mills. He first came to Estes Park in 1884 as a boy of fourteen. Five years later he met John Muir, who became his idol. He originally dreamed of a national park encompassing the forest from Estes Park to Pikes Peak. The political process was aided by James G. Rodgers of the Colorado Mountain Club and J. Horace MacFarland of the American Civic Association. Culmination of Mills' efforts was achieved on Jan. 26, 1915 when 358 sq. miles were established as Rocky Mountain National Park. This area was eventually enlarged to its present size of 413 sq. miles.

ROCKY MOUNTAIN

If all Rocky Mountain National Park had was Trail Ridge Road, it would be worth seeing. This road reaches an elevation of 12,183 ft., and for eleven miles it's above timberline, winding through the alpine tundra of delicate grasses and flowers. Some say it's like taking a ride on another planet; some feel they're passing through a lofty meadow touching the sky. Whatever the description or the feeling, all are touched by this unique and unforgettable experience. The road is closed in winter, but the Park's other roads remain open.

However, there is much more to the Park than Trail Ridge Road. The hiking is outstanding and the scenery spectacular. In the spring and summer wildflowers are abundant, and they, combined with the spectacular mountain peaks that hover above clear blue mountain lakes, make this park a photographer's paradise. It is "Colorful Colorado" at its best.

Sequoia

LOCATION:	East central California
ACCESS:	California 198 east from Visalia (35 mi.); Generals Highway via Kings Canyon National Park
SEASON:	All year (some roads closed in winter)
HOURS:	24 hours/day
ENTRANCE FEES:	$5/vehicle/week; $2/person all others/week; $15 annual; $25 Golden Eagle
FOOD:	Giant Forest and Three Rivers; store/deli at Lodgepole
GAS:	Lodgepole and Three Rivers, CA
NEAREST PROPANE:	Lodgepole and Three Rivers, CA
LODGING:	**Giant Forest Lodge:** ¼ mi. N of Giant Forest Village; motel, cabins & rustic cabins (some housekeeping); open all year except rustic cabins; reservations: Guest Services, Sequoia National Park, CA 93262; 209/561-3314
CAMPGROUNDS:	Seven campgrounds; reservations advised at Lodgepole; no hook-ups; trailers prohibited at Mineral King area and Buckeye Flat; group camping at Dorst
ADJACENT FACILITIES:	See below
VISITOR CENTERS:	Lodgepole Visitor Center; Ash Mountain Visitor Center
PICNICKING:	Designated areas throughout the Park
GIFT SHOPS:	Lodgepole; Giant Forest Lodge
TOURS:	Ranger-guided walks daily in summer; snowshoe walks weekends and holidays in winter; Crystal Caves tours
ACTIVITIES:	Hiking; fishing (license required); horseback riding; mountain climbing; alpine and cross-country skiing; interpretive programs
CLIMATE:	Hot summers with cool nights; snowy winters
ELEVATION:	1,700 ft. to 14,495 ft.
SIZE:	630 sq. miles
ANNUAL VISITATION:	Near one million
PETS:	Must be on leash; not allowed on trails
FACILITIES FOR DISABLED:	Campgrounds, restrooms, picnic areas
INFORMATION:	*Supt. Sequoia/Kings Canyon National Parks* *Three Rivers, CA 93271* 209/565-3341 *Emergency:* 911

- All campgrounds have tables, fireplaces and piped water.
- There is a camping limit of 14 days in summer; 30 days the remainder of the year.
- There are no hook-ups in the Park.
- Pay showers are available at Lodgepole and Stony Creek (summer only).
- Fishing is available at all campgrounds.
- Wood-gathering is permitted outside of sequoia groves; firewood is for sale in markets.

Giant Forest/Lodgepole Area

Lodgepole Village facilities include Visitor Center, post office, laundromat, gas station (minor repairs/propane), store, deli, bakery and gift shop.

Lodgepole (elev. 6700') is located 4 mi. NE of Giant Forest Village. It has 260 sites and is open all year (limited winter camping). The campground fee is $6 per night. This is the busiest campground in Sequoia and Kings Canyon and reservations are accepted up to 8 weeks in advance from any California Ticketron approximately mid-May through mid-September. Facilities include flush toilets, a dump station, amphitheater, telephone, and a camper store.

Dorst (elev. 6700') is located 12 mi. NW of Giant Forest Village. It has 238 individual sites, 7 group sites*, and is open late-June to Labor Day. The fee is $6 per night and campsites are on a first-come basis. Facilities include flush toilets and dump station. A general store and gas station are located within 4 miles.

*A fee of $1/night/person will be charged organized groups with 12 or more persons. For reservations: Dorst Campground Reservations, Box C—Lodgepole, Sequoia National Park, CA 93262.

Mineral King Area

Atwell Mill (elev. 6645') is located 20 mi. from Hammond Fire Station on Mineral King Road. It has 23 sites (TRAILERS PROHIBITED) and is open late May to late September. The campground fee is $4 per night. Facilities include pit toilets. A store is located within 2 miles at Silver City.

Cold Springs (elev. 7500') is located 24 mi. up Mineral King Road from Hwy. 198. It has 37 sites (TRAILERS PROHIBITED) and is open late May to late September. The campground fee is $4 per night. Facilities include pit toilets. A store is located within 3 miles at Silver City.

Lower Elevations

Potwisha (elev. 2100') is located 3 mi. above Park Headquarters. It has 44 sites (area designed for trailer parking) and is open all year. The campground fee is $6 per night. Facilities include flush toilets and a dump station.

Buckeye Flat (elev. 2800') is located 1 mi. from Hospital Rock Picnic Area. It has 28 sites (TRAILERS/RV'S PROHIBITED) and is closed in winter. The campground fee is $6 per night. Facilities include flush toilets.

South Fork (elev. 3600') is located 10 mi. E of Three Rivers on South Fork Road. It has 13 sites (not recommended for trailers) and is open all year. The fee is $4 per night. Facilities include pit toilets.

Bearpaw Meadow Camp: On a ridge at 7,800 ft. elevation; accessible only by 11-mile hike; open late June through early September; rustic tent cabins; dining tent

Stony Creek: (See Kings Canyon)

> *Reservations for above:* Guest Services, Sequoia National Park, CA 93262; 209/561-3314

Three Rivers Motel & Trailer Park: 2 mi. E of Three Rivers on Hwy. 198; open all year; full hook-ups; laundry; near store, cafe and ice; reservations: 43365 Sierra, Three Rivers, CA 93271; 209/561-4413

Silver City Store and Cabins: 3 mi. W of Mineral King Ranger Station on Mineral King Road; rustic cabins; groceries; showers; restaurant; reservations: Box 56, Three Rivers, CA 93271, 209/561-3223

Forest Service Campgrounds

Whitney Portal B: 12 mi. W of Lone Pine on CO 15502; open 5/15-10/31; 44 trailer or tent sites; flush toilets

Whitney Trailhead: 13 mi. W of Lone Pine on CO 15502; open 5/15-10-31; 8 tent and 10 trailer sites; flush toilets

Corps of Engineers Campground

Lake Kaweah: Located 20 mi. NE of Visalia on Hwy. 198; open all year; 10 tent and 70 trailer sites; flush toilets; showers

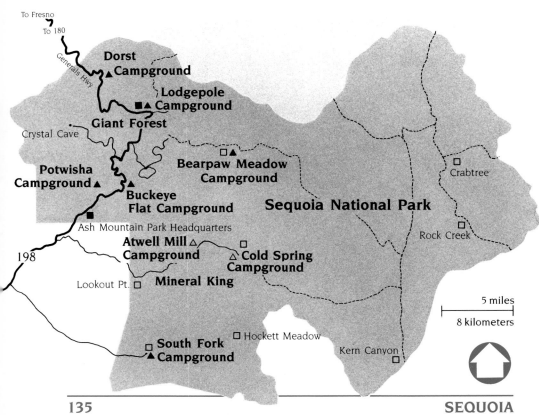

Giant Forest Area

Hazelwood Nature Trail: 1.0mi/1.6km loop; 1 hour; easy; trailhead: South side of Generals Hwy. opposite Giant Forest Lodge Registration Office. This gentle stroll through giant sequoia offers trailside exhibits and high reward for limited time and energy.

Huckleberry Meadow Loop: 5.0mi/8.0km loop; 3 hours; moderate; trailhead: South side of Generals Hwy. opposite Giant Forest Lodge Registration Office. This trail begins after a half-mile walk on the Hazelwood Nature Trail. Highlights of the trail include the Squatter's Cabin (built in 1880's), Huckleberry Meadow, impressive giant sequoias, and the Washington Tree, more than 30 ft. in diameter and 250 ft. tall.

Crescent Meadow/Log Meadow Loop: 1.8mi/2.9km loop; 2-3 hours; easy; trailhead: Crescent Meadow parking area. This trail follows a short section of the famous High Sierra Trail before skirting Crescent Meadow and a view of the Meadow from the south end, one of the best-known scenes in the Park. Near Log Meadow, with its abundance of wildflowers, is fire-hollowed Tharp's Log with an interpretive sign telling his story.

Congress Trail: 2.0mi/3.2km loop; 2-3 hours; easy; trailhead: General Sherman Tree. This self-guiding trail, the most popular of Giant Forest trails, offers a gentle walk through the impressive Congress Group area with its famous President and Chief Sequoyah Trees, the House and Senate Groups, etc. An interpretive pamphlet is available at the trailhead.

Trail of the Sequoias/Circle Meadow Loop: 6.0mi/9.6km loop; 4 hours; moderate; trailhead: General Sherman Tree. This trail follows and then parallels the Congress Trail before ascending a sequoia-shaded route to Crescent Creek, then Log Meadow, Tharp's Log, Chimney Tree, Circle Meadow, and returning to Congress Grove.

Moro Rock/Soldiers Trail Loop: 4.6mi/7.4km loop; 3-4 hours; moderate; trailhead: Giant Forest Village west of cafeteria. This trail offers beautiful groves of giant sequoias on route to Moro Rock. The vistas are spectacular from the summit of the monolith with much of Sequoia Park visible and sometimes even the Coast Ranges 100 miles away. Return is by numerous famous giant sequoias and the historic site of Soldiers Camp.

Lodgepole/Wolverton Area

The Tokopah Trail: 1.7mi/2.7km one way; easy; ascent 500'; trailhead: Lodgepole Campground. This trail follows the banks of the Marble Fork of the Kaweah River offering a story of glacial erosion, a profusion of wildflowers during summer, wildlife, a walk through the "High Sierra", and concludes at the base of the 1200-ft. high Tokopah Falls.

The Lakes Trail: To Heather Lake 4.6mi/7.4km; to Emerald Lake 5.7mi/9.1km; to Pear Lake 6.7mi/10.7km (all one way via Watchtower Trail); strenuous; ascent 2,300'; trailhead: Wolverton parking area. This is the most popular backcountry trail in the Park with Pear Lake a popular base camp for hiking beyond the trails. Fishing and swimming are enjoyed at Heather Lake and camping at Emerald Lake. "The Watchtower" offers spectacular vistas of the Valley 1600 ft. below and the alpine ridges to the north and east.

The Alta Peak/Alta Meadow Trails: To Panther Gap 2.7mi/4.3km; to Mehrten Meadow 4.0mi/6.4km; to Alta Meadow 5.7mi/9.1km; to Alta Peak 6.9mi/11.0km (all one way); strenuous to Alta Meadow; ascent 2100'; very strenuous to Alta Peak; ascent 4,000'; trailhead: Wolverton parking area. This trail follows the Lakes Trail part way to Panther Gap, where the Kaweah River can be viewed in the canyon 5,000 feet below. The trail intersects the Seven-Mile-Hill Trail and the High Sierra Trail en route to Mehrten Meadow, a popular camping area. Scenic Alta Meadow offers carpets of wildflowers and views of the Great Western Divide. Alta Peak, at elevation 11,204, provides a spectacular 360 degree panorama of lakes, peaks, valleys, and, through a gap in the Great Western Divide, even Mt. Whitney.

The Twin Lakes Trail: To Silliman Creek 2.1mi/3.4km; to Clover Creek 5.0mi/8.0km; to Twin Lakes 6.8mi/10.9km; strenuous; ascent 2,700'; trailhead: Lodgepole Campground. The appeal of this trail is the lush environment along the way, the wildflowers and wildlife, and beautiful, tree-lined Twin Lakes. The trail continues steeply to the summit of Silliman Pass (Silliman Crest) (1.5mi/2.4km) and the boundary of Kings Canyon National Park.

Mineral King Area

Timber Gap Trail: 2.0mi/3.2km one way; ascent 1,400'; trailhead: Sawtooth Pass parking area. This trail follows Monarch Creek and an old mining route, then climbs steeply through a dense forest to a clearing of wildflowers and views of Alta Peak and into the valley north.

Monarch Lakes Trail: 4.2mi/6.7km one way; ascent 2,580'; trailhead: Sawtooth Pass parking area. This trail ascends to Groundhog Meadow and then, via a series of switchbacks through a red fir forest, to Lower Monarch Lake where camping is allowed with a wilderness permit. Upper Monarch Lake is ¼ mile to

the southeast and Sawtooth Pass, with its spectacular vistas, is a 1200 ft. climb for another 1.3 miles.

Crystal Lake Trail: 4.9mi/7.8km one way; ascent 3,000'; trailhead: Sawtooth Pass parking lot. This trail branches from the Monarch Lakes Trail 3.2 miles from the trailhead, crosses the Chihuahua Bowl, and ascends steeply to Crystal Lake with panoramic views along the way. There are campsites at Crystal Lake, and Little Crystal Lake is just a short way up the bluffs to the northeast.

Franklin Lakes Trail: 5.4mi/8.6km one way; ascent 2,527'; trailhead: Eagle-Mosquito parking area. This trail encompasses walking an old abandoned road, boulder-hopping across Crystal Creek, crossing Franklin Creek twice, and ascending through multicolored rock up the steep valley created by Franklin Creek.

White Chief Trail: To Bowl 2.9mi/4.6km one way; to Valley's end 4.1mi/6.6km one way; ascent to Bowl 1,400'; ascent to Valley's end 2,200'; trailhead: Eagle-Mosquito parking area. The trail to White Chief Canyon is a steep and scenic one. It passes "mysterious" Spring Creek, ascends rocky bluffs to White Chief meadows, climbs to the old White Chief Mine, and, beyond, eventually disappears in the giant glacial cirque that forms the head of the Canyon.

Eagle Lake Trail: 3.4mi/5.4km one way; ascent 2,200'; trailhead: Eagle-Mosquito parking area. This trail follows the White Chief Trail for a mile, then proceeds towards Eagle Canyon, where wildflowers are varied and abundant during early summer. The trail proceeds past where Eagle Creek "disappears" into a big hole, a densely forested area and a boulder field before arriving at this glacially-formed lake.

Mosquito Lake #1: 3.6mi/5.8km one way; ascent 1,190'; trailhead: Eagle-Mosquito parking area. This trail shares the White Chief Trail and Eagle Lake Trail for 1 mile, then proceeds over Miner's Ridge and drops to Mosquito Lake. The trail ends mid-way up the Lake, but the other four lakes may be hiked to for trout fishing or just enjoyment.

BRIEF HISTORY

See Kings Canyon National Park.

AUTHOR'S COMMENTS

SEQUOIA. The word says it all. The largest living things on earth are awesome to behold. Their immense size dwarfs us and, seen together in a grove, establishes a feeling of reverence and wonder. Nearly two million people a year come to see these groves, and I never heard anyone say, "If you've seen one Sequoia, you've seen them all"

Yellowstone

LOCATION: Northwestern Wyoming

ACCESS: From east on Hwy. 14-16-20 from Cody, WY; from south on Hwy. 287 from Grand Teton; from northeast on Hwy. 212 from Silver Gate; from northeast on Hwy. 89 from Gardiner; from west on Hwy. 20 from West Yellowstone.

SEASON: Road within Park from North Entrance to Cooke City open all year; all other entrances closed to automobiles in winter

HOURS: 24 hours/day

ENTRANCE FEES: $5/vehicle/week (includes admission to Grand Teton); $2/person all others/week; $15 annual; $25 Golden Eagle

GAS & FOOD: Fishing Bridge; Mammoth Hot Springs; Tower-Roosevelt; Old Faithful; Grant Village; Canyon Village; Lake Village; Bridge Bay

NEAREST PROPANE: At gas stations throughout Park

CAMPGROUNDS: 12 NPS campgrounds plus one concessioner-operated RV trailer park with hook-ups (see Campgrounds section for reservation information)

LODGING: Lake Village; Mammoth Hot Springs; Tower-Roosevelt; Old Faithful; Grant Village; Canyon Village (see Accommodations section for reservation information)

ADJACENT FACILITIES:
• In Gardner Mt.—just north of Park Boundary on Hwy. 89
• In West Yellowstone—just west of Park Boundary on Hwy. 20
• In Cooke City and Silvergate—at Northeast Entrance
• In Cody, WY—approximately 60 miles east of Park Boundary on Hwy. 20
• In Jackson—approximately 60 miles south of Park Boundary on Hwy. 89
• Numerous Forest Service campgrounds on all highways surrounding the Park

VISITOR CENTERS: Old Faithful; Grant Village; Fishing Bridge; Canyon Village; Mammoth Hot Springs

MUSEUMS: Norris and Madison; exhibits at most Visitor Centers

PICNICKING: Throughout the Park (many areas with tables and restrooms but not drinking water)

GIFT SHOPS: Fishing Bridge; Mammoth Hot Springs; Grant Village; Old Faithful; Tower-Roosevelt; Lake Village; Canyon Village

TOURS: Ranger-led hikes and walks during summer; bus and boat tours; ski and snowmobile tours in winter

ACTIVITIES: Hiking; backpacking; cross-country skiing and snowmobiling; fishing; horseback riding; boating; stagecoach rides; interpretive programs

CLIMATE:	Mild days and cool to cold nights in summer; heavy snowfall and to below freezing in winter
ELEVATION:	5,314 to 11,358 ft.
SIZE:	3,472 sq. miles
ANNUAL VISITATION:	Between two and two-and-a-half million
PETS:	Allowed on leash except on trails and boardwalks, in backcountry and in public buildings
FACILITIES FOR DISABLED:	All public areas; some interpretive areas; guidebook available at visitor centers
INFORMATION:	*Supt. Yellowstone National Park* *P.O. Box 168* *Yellowstone National Park, WY 82190* *307/344-7381* *Park Emergency: 911 or 344-7381*

CAMPGROUNDS

• All campsites are available on a first-come basis except concessioner-operated trailer park, where reservations are possible.

• All opening and closing dates are approximate due to snow depth, availability of water, availability of personnel to maintain facilities, etc.

• Most campgrounds fill by mid- to late-afternoon in summer, and some earlier in July and August.

• All camping limited to 7 days July through Labor Day, 30 days Labor Day through June.

• Dead and down firewood may be gathered, and wood is for sale at convenient locations in the park.

• Fishing is available from all of the campgrounds (non-fee fishing permit required).

• Group camping is available May through September; reservations: 307/344-7381

• *There are special regulations in the campgrounds designed to prevent bears from obtaining food; a list of rules is available at the campgrounds.*

Bridge Bay (elev. 7784') is located 3 mi. S of Lake Village in a largely open area with lodgepole pine forest. It has 420 sites and is open May to October. Facilities include tables and grills, flush toilets, piped water, amphitheatre, wood for sale, and a dump station. The campground fee is $6 per night. Showers and laundry facilities are available in nearby Fishing Bridge. There is a store, boat launching facilities and boat rentals near the campground. The campground has handicapped access.

Canyon (elev. 7734') is located ¼ mi. E of Canyon Junction in a reasonably level area with a lodgepole pine forest. *The campground is restricted to "hard-sided" vehicles only* (no tents or tent trailers). It has 280 sites and is open June to September. Facilities include tables and grills, flush toilets, piped water, amphitheater, wood for sale, and a dump station. The campground is self-registration and the fee is $6. Showers and laundry facilities are available nearby as well as a store, gas station, post office, restaurant, lodging, ranger station and public telephones. Boating and fishing are also available.

Fishing Bridge (elev. 7784') is located 1 mi. E of Fishing Bridge Junction in a level area of lodgepole pine. *The campground is restricted to "hard-sided" vehicles only* (no tents or tent trailers). It has 308 sites and is open June to September. Facilities include tables and grills, flush toilets, piped water, wood for sale, and a dump station. The campground is self-registration and the fee is $6. Showers and laundry facilities are available in nearby Fishing Bridge Village.

Grant Village (elev. 7733') is located 2 mi. S of West Thumb Junction in a nice environment. It has 403 sites and is open June to October. Facilities include tables and grills, flush toilets, piped water nearby, amphitheater, and a dump station. The campground is self-registration and the fee is $6. Services adjacent to the campground include laundry facilities, showers, store, post office, ice, visitor center, service station, restaurant, ranger station, lodging and boat launch.

Indian Creek (elev. 7200') is located 7½ mi. S of Mammoth Junction in a lodgepole pine forest. It has 75 sites suitable for tents or small trailers and is open June through September. Facilities include piped water and pit toilets, grills and a campfire circle with nightly programs most summers. The campground fee is $5 per night.

Lewis Lake (elev. 7500') is located 10 mi. S of West Thumb. It has 85 sites and is open June through October. Facilities include piped water, pit toilets, and grills. The campground fee is $5 per night. Other facilities include a ranger station and a boat launch.

Madison (elev. 6800') is located ¼ mi. W of Madison Junction. It has 292 sites and is open May through October. Facilities include tables and grills, flush toilets, piped water and a sanitary dump station. The campground fee is $6 per night. Other facilities include a ranger station and a museum. The campground is accessible for handicapped.

Mammoth (elev. 6239′) is located ½ mi. N of Mammoth Junction in a relatively open area. It has 85 sites, with some reserved for hikers and bicyclers, and is the only campground in the Park open all year. Facilities include tables and grills, flush toilets, piped water, an amphitheater with programs various evenings, and firewood for sale in summer. The campground fee is $6 per night. Facilities in nearby Mammoth Hot Springs include a store, lodging, gas station, restaurant, post office, medical clinic, chapel, visitor center and Park Headquarters.

Norris (elev. 7484′) is located 1 mi. N of Norris Junction in a lodgepole pine forest adjacent to a meadow with a stream. It has 116 sites suitable for tents or smaller RV's and is open May through September. Facilities include tables and grills, flush toilets, piped water, campfire circle, telephones, and firewood for sale. The campground fee is $6 per night. There is a ranger station and a museum at the Geyser Basin within a mile of the campground.

Pebble Creek (elev. 7300′) is located 7 mi. S of Northeast Entrance. It has 36 sites and is open June to September. Facilities include grills, piped water and pit toilets. The campground fee is $5 per night.

Slough Creek (elev. 6300′) is located 10 mi. SE of Tower Junction. It has 29 sites and is open May through October. Facilities include some tables and grills and pit toilets. The campground fee is $5 per night.

Tower Fall (elev. 6270′) is located 3 mi. SE of Tower Junction in a lodgepole pine forested area. It has 32 sites suitable for tents or small trailers and is open June through September. Facilities include some tables and grills, piped water and pit toilets. The campground fee is $5 per night. Facilities in nearby Tower Junction include a store, lodging, restaurant, gas station, and ranger station. Activities include horseback riding.

Fishing Bridge Recreational Vehicle Park (elev. 7700′) is located 1½ mi. E of Lake Junction. It has 358 sites, is open June to September and provides full hook-ups for RV's up to 40 feet. No tents or pop-ups are allowed. The fee is $11 per night. For reservations write TW Services, Inc., Yellowstone Nat'l Park, Wyo. 82190-9989, 307/344-7311.

ACCOMMODATIONS

A wide variety of concessioner-operated accommodations are available at six geographical areas within the Park: Mammoth Hot Springs, Tower-Roosevelt, Canyon Village, Yellowstone Lake, Grant Village, and Old Faithful. For details or reservations: TW Services, Inc., c/o Reservations, Yellowstone National Park, Wyo. 82190-9989; 307/344-7311 (room reservations); 307/344-7901, ext. 5240 (activities reservations).

HIKING

There are over 1,000 miles of trails in Yellowstone National Park. Suggested reading for details are the following: *Yellowstone Trails* by Mark C. Marschall, *Day Hiking* by Tom Carter, *Hiking the Backcountry* by Orville E. Bach, Jr., and *The Sierra Club Guide to National Parks* (*Rocky Mountains and the Great Plains*). In addition, most visitor centers have free pamphlets on suggested hikes in its particular area.

Self-guiding Trails include the following, with trail guides available at visitor centers and trailheads: *For your own safety, it is imperative that you stay on designated trails and boardwalks in thermal areas and near the rims of the Grand Canyon.*

Upper Geyser Basin: The trailhead is at the Old Faithful Visitor Center. This largely boardwalk trail explores the greatest concentration of geyser and hot springs activity in the world.

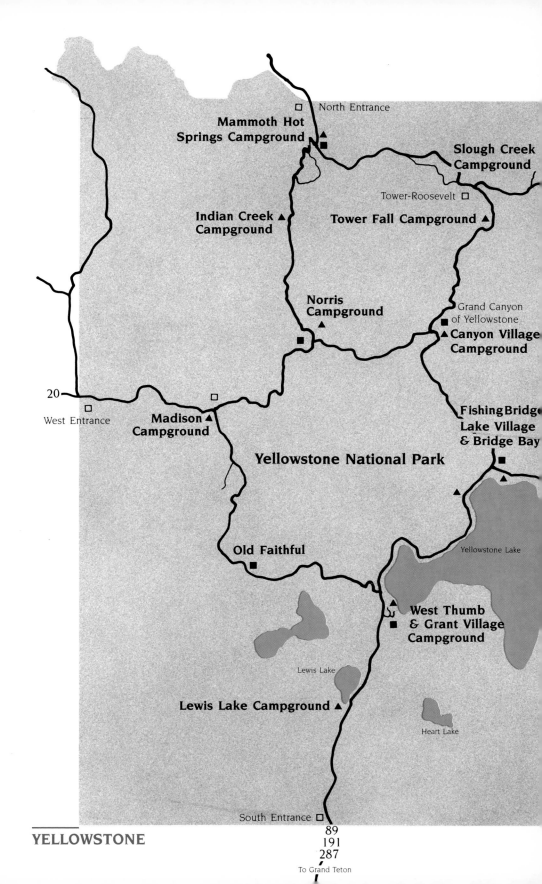

North Entrance

Mammoth Hot
Springs Campground

Slough Creek
Campground

Tower-Roosevelt

Indian Creek
Campground

Tower Fall Campground

Norris
Campground

Grand Canyon
of Yellowstone

Canyon Village
Campground

20

West Entrance

Madison
Campground

Fishing Bridge
Lake Village
& Bridge Bay

Yellowstone National Park

Old Faithful

Yellowstone Lake

West Thumb
& Grant Village
Campground

Lewis Lake

Lewis Lake Campground

Heart Lake

South Entrance

YELLOWSTONE

89
191
287
To Grand Teton

Fountain Paint Pot Nature Trail: The trailhead is located half-way between Madison Junction and Old Faithful. The trail winds through steam vents, mud pots and hot springs. *Three Senses* self-guiding trail is also in this area.

Northeast Entrance

212

Norris Geyser Basin: The trailhead is at the Norris Museum. The trail leads into the hottest, most changeable geyser basin in Yellowstone (and the world).

▲ **Pebble Creek Campground**

Mammoth Hot Springs Terraces: The trailhead is off the "Grand Loop Road". Boardwalks wind through active and inactive areas in this constantly changing scene.

Grand Canyon of Yellowstone: The trailheads are the parking lots off road at Canyon Village. Roads and trails along the north and south rims of the canyon lead to overlooks of Lower and Upper Falls and spectacular views of colored formations.

Mud Volcano: The trailhead is off the Park road 10 miles south of Canyon Junction and 6 miles north of Fishing Bridge Junction. The trail winds past bubbling, mudhissing fumaroles.

BRIEF HISTORY

Native Americans have inhabited the area ever since the last Ice Age ended some 8500 years ago. The Blackfeet, Crow, Shoshone and others were all visitors to the area; however, the only permanent residents were the Tukudikas (Sheepeaters), a rather passive tribe.

⌐ **Campgrounds**

As in Grand Teton National Park, the first explorer was probably John Colter, who left the Lewis and Clark Expedition on its return east in the winter of 1807-08. Rumors founded by trappers and mountain men told of a wondrous land of rivers, waterfalls, geysers, thermal activity and spectacular scenery. These rumors were confirmed by three expeditions. First there was the Folsom, Cook, and Peterson Expedition in 1869, and second was the Washburn, Langford and Doane Expedition in 1870. Then followed the F. V. Hayden geological and geographical survey of 1871. With strong support from Northern Pacific Railroad, the political climate was ripe and Yellowstone, the "Grand Daddy", the world's first national park, was established March 1, 1872. Establishing the Park was one thing; funding money for its administration was another. As a result of lack of funds, the Park lacked proper administration and protection for its many visitors. The army took over in 1886 and administered it until 1918, when the National Park Service assumed the administrative responsibilities.

16
14

5 miles

8 kilometers

If you approach Yellowstone National Park from the east, plan to visit the "Buffalo Bill" Museum in Cody, WY. Among other things, it has probably the best exhibit of the Plains Indians that exists. The visit will provide you with a feel of the old west that will enable you to enjoy Yellowstone to the fullest.

There's a lot to see in Yellowstone—it's a big park (3472 sq. miles). The scenery, thermal activity or wildlife by itself would qualify it as a national park, and when it's all combined, it's overwhelming. The thing that impressed me most was the wildlife. On a northern loop six-hour drive from Fishing Bridge, I saw grizzly bear and 2 cubs, bison, pelicans, geese, bull and cow elk, coyote, bull cow and calf moose, deer and pronghorn. (I also saw 1,000 RV's with a top speed of 20 mph.) I'm sure with a trained eye, I would have seen more (not RV's but wildlife).

Yellowstone was the world's first national park, and, as such, the National Park Service has had to write the book, so to speak. Naturally some mistakes have been made. The Park Service has had a difficult job trying to protect the environment on one hand and provide tourist facilities on the other. Wildlife and large numbers of people don't usually mix well. Scientific research into the effects of man on the environment is a top priority item for the Park Service. I personally feel that Yellowstone is an example of the National Park Service doing its job with a great deal of skill.

I wish I had more time to enjoy Yellowstone, and I'm sure you will feel that way too.

Yosemite

LOCATION: East central California

ACCESS: From Fresno, 59 mi. to South Entrance via CA 41; from Merced, 67 mi. to Arch Rock Entrance via CA 140; from Oakdale, 71 mi. to Big Oak Flat Road via CA 120; from junction of CA 120 and US 395 (only entrance from the east), 12 mi. to Tioga Pass Entrance via CA 120 (closed east of Crane Flat approximately early Nov. to Memorial Day weekend)

SEASON: All year

HOURS: 24 hours/day

ENTRANCE FEES: $5/vehicle/week; $2/person all others/week; $15 annual; $25 Golden Eagle

FOOD & LODGING: Year-round in Yosemite Valley; summer only at Wawona Hotel, Tuolumne Meadows and White Wolf (see Accommodations below)

GAS: Year-round in Yosemite Valley and at Wawona; summer only at Crane Flat and Tuolumne Meadows

NEAREST PROPANE: Yosemite Valley Service Station

CAMPGROUNDS: All campgrounds in Yosemite Valley except Sunnyside and Backpackers Walk-in Campgrounds on Ticketron spring to fall (inclusive dates variable); also Hodgdon Meadow on Hwy. 120 at Big Oak Flat Entrance; others in park (9) on first-come basis; 4 are open year-round; no hook-ups; group camps in Valley, Hodgdon Meadow, Tuolumne Meadows on Ticketron

ADJACENT FACILITIES: Numerous motels, RV parks, lodges, and cabins on all access highways (see below)

VISITOR CENTERS: Yosemite Valley Visitor Center (year-round): Tuolumne Meadows Visitor Center (summer only); Big Oak Flat Information Station (summer only)

MUSEUMS: In Yosemite Valley: Indian Cultural Museum, LeConte Memorial Lodge, Happy Isles Nature Center, and exhibits in Visitor Center; at Wawona: Pioneer Yosemite History Center; in the Mariposa Grove: Mariposa Grove Museum

PICNICKING: Throughout park in designated areas

GIFT SHOPS: Yosemite Lodge, Yosemite Village, Ahwahnee Hotel (all year-round); Curry Village, Wawona Hotel, Glacier Point, Mariposa Grove (all summer only)

TOURS: Ranger-guided walks and hikes; saddle trips; tram tours

ACTIVITIES: Hiking; backpacking; swimming; boating (motorless craft only); fishing (license required); bicycling; wildlife-watching; horseback riding; mountain climbing; skiing (downhill and cross-country); rock- and ice-climbing schools; photography classes; numerous ranger-conducted activities; Yosemite Theater with performing and film arts programs

CLIMATE: Pleasant days with cool nights and occasional thunderstorms in summer; usually heavy snow pack in winter at 6000' and higher; some snow at lower elevations

ELEVATION: 2,000 to 13,114 ft.

SIZE: 1,190 sq. miles

ANNUAL VISITATION: Near three million

PETS: Must be on leash; not permitted on trails, in backcountry or public buildings; permitted in designated campgrounds only; kennels available approximately April through October

FACILITIES FOR DISABLED: General information packet available at entrances and visitor centers describing numerous facilities and services

INFORMATION: *Supt. Yosemite National Park*
P.O. Box 577
Yosemite National Park, CA 95389
209/372-0264
Park Emergency: 911
Road conditions: 209/372-4605

CAMPGROUNDS

• All campgrounds provide tables, tent space, tap water, flush toilets (except Porcupine Flat, Yosemite Creek and Tamarack Flat), fire pits or grills.
• There are no hook-ups in the campgrounds.
• All opening and closing dates are approximate depending on weather and use.
• Dead and down firewood gathering is permitted.
• Pets must be on leash and are restricted to Bridalveil Creek, Crane Flat, Hodgdon Meadow, Tuolumne Meadows, Upper Pines, Wawona, White Wolf and Yosemite Creek Campgrounds.
• Fishing is permitted with a California fishing license.
• The following apply to *Yosemite Valley* campgrounds:
　　All are at elevation 4000'.
　　All have a 7-day limit of stay except Backpackers (2-day limit) 6/1-9/15 (all other campgrounds have 14-day limit of stay 6/1-9/15 and 30-day limit of stay rest of year).
　　All are on Ticketron about 4/8-11/28 (inclusive dates variable year-to-year) with the exception of Sunnyside (walk-in), Backpackers (walk-in) and Organization Group (reservations accepted). Ticketron information: Up to 8 weeks in advance, in person at any Ticketron outlet or by mail, or in Yosemite Valley, or write Ticketron, Dept. R, (Reservations), 401 Hackensack Ave., Hackensack, NJ 07601. Group camp reservations may be made up to 12 weeks in advance. (All other campgrounds are on a first-come basis).
　　All are near showers, laundry, stores, gas, propane, post office, gift shops, restaurants, medical and dental facilities, beauty/barber shop, bank, auto repair, babysitting, stables, film development, and religious services. For details see the free ''Yosemite Guide''.

All have access to fishing and all have horseback riding available except Sunnyside and Backpacker.

All are served by free shuttle bus service when they're open.

Yosemite Valley Campgrounds

Sunnyside is a walk-in campground located directly across from Yosemite

Lodge. It has 38 spaces, is open all year, and the fee is $2/person/night. The campground is heavily used by rock climbers spring and fall and as an overflow campground, so it is usually full except for winter months.

Upper Pines has 240 sites, is open approximately 4/1-10/31, and the fee is $10 per night. Facilities include a dump station.

Lower Pines is located at Stop 19 on the shuttle bus system. It has 173 sites, some to accommodate large trailers, is open approximately 4/1-10/31, and the fee is $10 per night. Facilities for disabled visitors are available.

Upper River is a tents-only campground. It has 124 sites, is open approximately 5/1-11/30, and the fee is $10 per night.

Lower River is located across the road from Upper River Campground. It has 139 sites, is open year-round, and the fee is $10 per night. Facilities include a dump station.

North Pines has 85 sites, is open approximately 5/1-10/15,and the fee is $10 per night

Backpackers is a walk-in campground located across the creek from North Pines. It has 25 sites, is open approximately 5/27-10/1, and the fee is $2/person/night.

Organization Group has 11 group sites (limited to 30 persons per site), is open approximately 5/1-10/1, and the fee is $33/site. For reservations, contact Ticketron.

Campgrounds not in Yosemite Valley

Bridalveil Creek (elev. 7200') is located on the Glacier Point Road 22 mi. from Yosemite Valley in a lodgepole pine forest. It has 110 sites (some suitable for large trailers), is open approximately 6/10-10/1, and the fee is $6 per night. The campground usually fills by 2 p.m. in summer.

Crane Flat (elev. 6190') is located on Hwy. 120 west near the Tioga Road turn-off 16 mi. from Yosemite Valley in a forest of white fir, lodgepole pine and ponderosa pine. It has 129 sites, is open approximately 5/30-10/1, and the fee is $6 per night. A grocery store is nearby. The campground usually fills by 2 p.m. in summer.

Hodgdon Meadow (elev. 4872') is located on Hwy. 120 west near the Big Oak Flat Entrance 25 mi. from Yosemite Valley in a forested area. It has 107 individual sites (some suitable for large trailers), 6 group sites, is open all year, and the fee is $9 per night. This campground will be on Ticketron reservation system from 4/8-11/28.

Porcupine Flat (elev. 8100') is located on Hwy. 120 east 6 mi. W of Tenaya Lake and 38 mi. from Yosemite Valley in a lodgepole pine forest. It has 52 sites, is open approximately 6/10-10/15, and the fee is $3 per night.

Tamarack Flat (elev. 6315') is located just off Hwy. 120 east 6 mi. E of Crane Flat 22 mi. from Yosemite Valley. It has 52 sites, is open approximately 6/10-10/15, and the fee is $3 per night.

Tenaya Lake (elev. 7600') is a walk-in campground located on Hwy. 120 east at the west end of Tenaya Lake 46 mi. from Yosemite Valley. It has 50 sites, is open approximately 6/10-10/15, and the fee is $6 per night. Swimming and fishing are available in the lake.

Tuolumne Meadows (elev. 8600') is located 29 mi. from the junction of US 395 on Hwy. 120 east 55 mi. from Yosemite Valley in a forest of lodgepole pine. It has 325 sites, is open approximately 6/10-10/15, and the fee is $6 per night. A dump station is located near the visitor center. A grocery store and showers are available, as well as fishing, horseback riding, and a mountaineering school. The campground usually fills in summer but often has space available in spring and fall. It serves as trailhead for numerous day hikes, including Dog Lake, Elizabeth Lake, Glen Aulin, Cathedral Lakes and Lembert Dome.

Tuolumne Backpackers (elev. 8600') is a walk-in campground located .6 mi. E of Tuolumne Meadows Campground. It has 25 sites, is open approximately 6/10-10/15, and the fee is $1/person/night.

Wawona (elev. 4000') is located on Hwy. 41 6 mi. N of South Entrance 27 mi. from Yosemite Valley in a wooded area with lower level sites adjacent to a river. It has 100 individual sites and one group site, is open all year, and the fee is $6 per night. A store is available, as well as swimming, fishing, and horseback riding.

White Wolf (elev. 8000') is located on Hwy. 120 east 31 mi. from Yosemite Valley. It has 86 sites, is open approximately 6/10-9/15, and the fee is $6 per night. A small camp store, fishing, and horseback riding are available.

Yosemite Creek (elev. 7659') is located on Hwy. 120 east 35 mi. from Yosemite Valley. It has 75 sites, is open approximately June-Oct., and the fee is $3 per night. Fishing is available.

ACCOMMODATIONS

For *reservations/information* for all the following accommodations in Yosemite, contact the Yosemite Park and Curry Company Reservations, 5410 E. Home, Fresno, CA 93727; 209/252-4848 (hearing impaired TTY 209/255-8345).

The Ahwahnee: in Yosemite Valley; open all year; listed in National Register of Historic Places; most luxurious accommodation in the park; 99 rooms and 24 cottages all with private baths; formal dining (with dress code for dinner); cocktail lounge; game room; pool; tennis courts; gift shop; babysitting.

Yosemite Lodge: in Yosemite Valley; open all year; 226 lodge rooms with private baths and 139 cabins, most with private baths; restaurants; cafeteria; lounge; bar; gift shop; bicycle rentals; post office; pool; evening interpretive programs.

Curry Village: near the base of Glacier Point in Yosemite Valley; open all year; 18 lodge rooms, 173 rustic cabins, 408 tent cabins (spring through fall); cafeteria; hamburger stand; ice cream stand; pool; gift shop; sporting goods; cocktail patio; bicycle rentals; ice skating rink (winter); amphitheater with evening interpretive programs (summer).

Wawona Hotel: 6 mi. from South Entrance to park; open Easter through Thanksgiving; listed in National Register of Historic Places; 66 rooms, most with private baths; 9-hole golf course; tennis courts; pool; stables; formal dining with dress code for dinner; nature trails.

Housekeeping Camp: ½ mi. S of Yosemite Village; open approximately Memorial Day through Labor Day; 300 concrete and canvas tent-cabins; store; laundry; bath/shower complex.

Tuolumne Meadows: Canvas tent cabins; dining hall; showers; stables nearby.

White Wolf: Cabins and canvas tent cabins; dining hall; showers; stables.

NOTE: Mileage given is from Yosemite Valley Visitor Center.

Along Highway 140 toward Merced

El Portal: 14 mi.; motels, RV parks and lodges

USFS C.G.—*Indian Flat*: located 24 mi. NE of Marisposa on Hwy. 140; open approximately 5/15-11/1

Midpines: 36 mi.; motels

KOA *Yosemite—Mariposa*: 7 mi. NE of Mariposa on Hwy. 140; open all year; full hook-ups; showers; flush toilets; propane, dump station; store; laundry; ice; reservations: 6323 Hwy. 140, Midpines, CA 95345, 209/966-2201

Mariposa: 43 mi.; motels, bed & breakfasts; lodges and youth hostel

Along Highway 41 toward Fresno

Yosemite West: 16 mi.; condominiums, cottages, mountain homes

Wawona: 27 mi.; cabins, cottages, motel, Wawona Hotel

Fish Camp: 36 mi.; chalets, inn, lodges

USFS C.G.—*Little Sandy*: .5 mi. S of Fish Camp on Hwy. 41, 6.9 mi. E on FR 6S00; open approximately 6/1-10/31

USFS C.G.—*Summerdale*: .6 mi. N of Fish Camp on Hwy. 41, 5 mi. N on FR 5S50; open approximately 5/20-10/31

USFS C.G.—*Big Sandy*: .5 mi. S of Fish Camp on Hwy. 41, 5.3 mi. E on FR 6S00; open approximately 6/1-10/31.

Along Highway 120 east toward Lee Vining

Tioga Pass Resort: 2 mi. E of Tioga Pass Entrance Station and 65 mi. from Yosemite Valley; open approximately 6/1-9/30; cabins; gas; food; reservations: P.O. Box 7, Lee Vining, CA 93541.

USFS C.G.—*Tioga Lake*: 1 mi. E of Tioga Pass Entrance Station on CA 120; open approximately 6/1-10/15; 13 tent sites; near store, cafe, ice.

USFS C.G.—*Ellery Lake*: 2 mi. E of Tioga Pass Entrance Station on CA 120; open approximately 6/1-10/15; 13 tent sites, 5 trailer sites; flush toilets; near store, cafe, ice.

USFS C.G.—*Saddlebag Lake*: 1.5 mi. E of Tioga Pass Entrance Station on CA 120, 2 mi. NW on CO 1N04; open approximately 6/1-10/15; 22 tent and trailer sites; near store, cafe, ice.

Lee Vining: 12 mi. E of Tioga Pass Entrance Station near junction of CA 120 and US 395; 74 mi. from Yosemite Valley; motels; lodges; restaurants.

County Campground Lee Vining Creek: 5 mi. W of junction of CA 120 and US 395; open approximately 5/15-10/15.

County Campground Aspen Grove: 7 mi. N of junction of CA 120 and US 395; open approximately 5/15-10/15.

Along Highway 120 west toward Manteca

Between Big Oak Flat Entrance and Groveland: lodges; motels; RV park.

USFS C.G.—*Middle Fork*: located 20.7 mi. E of Groveland on Hwy. 120, 4.5 mi. N on CO 3400; open approximately 5/1-11/1.

USFS C.G.—*Lost Claim*: located 10.6 mi. E of Groveland on Hwy 120; open approximately 4/1-11/1.

HIKING

There are more than 750mi/1200km of trails in Yosemite. Backcountry overnight hiking requires a free permit available at visitor centers and ranger stations throughout the park. Some of the more popular trails are listed below. For more detailed information on hikes, there are numerous books and pamphlets for sale as well as Park Service literature available at visitor centers and ranger stations.

From Yosemite Valley

Lower Yosemite Fall: .75mi/1.25km from Valley Visitor Center to base of fall; .25mi/ .4km from Lower Fall shuttle bus stop to base of fall; 1 hr. roundtrip from Visitor Center; 20 min. roundtrip from shuttle bus stop; easy; wheelchair accessible with assistance; trailhead: Yosemite Fall parking area and shuttle bus stop. This walk follows a paved trail to the bridge at the base of Lower Yosemite Fall.

Bridalveil Fall: .25mi/.4km to base of fall; 20 min. roundtrip; easy; wheelchair accessible with assistance; trailhead: Bridalveil Fall parking area. This walk follows a paved trail to base of fall. Expect to get wet from the mist in the spring; rainbows can sometimes be seen in the fall in late afternoon.

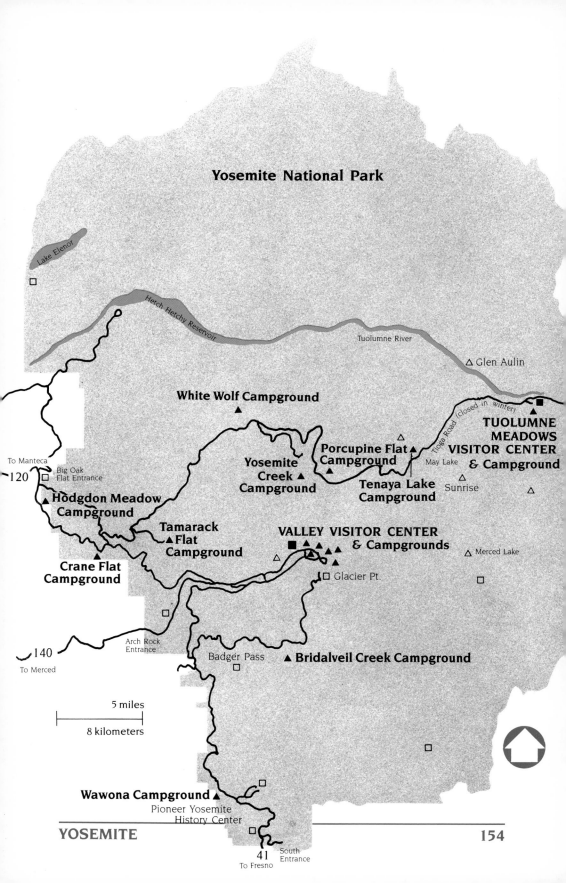

Yosemite National Park

Lake Elenor

Hetch Hetchy Reservoir

Tuolumne River

△ Glen Aulin

White Wolf Campground ▲

Tioga Road (closed in winter)

TUOLUMNE MEADOWS VISITOR CENTER ■

Porcupine Flat Campground ▲ △

Yosemite Creek Campground ▲

May Lake

& Campground

To Manteca

△ Sunrise △

120 Big Oak Flat Entrance □

Tenaya Lake Campground ▲

▲ **Hodgdon Meadow Campground**

Tamarack Flat Campground ▲

VALLEY VISITOR CENTER ■ ▲ ▲ ▲ ▲ ▲ **& Campgrounds**

△ Merced Lake

△

Crane Flat Campground

□ Glacier Pt. □

Arch Rock Entrance

140

To Merced

Badger Pass □ ▲ **Bridalveil Creek Campground**

5 miles

8 kilometers

□

Wawona Campground ▲

Pioneer Yosemite History Center

□

□

41

South Entrance

To Fresno

Mirror Lake: 1.0mi/1.6km to lake; 3.0mi/4.8km loop around lake; ½ hr. to lake; 2 hrs. around lake; easy; wheelchair accessible to lake with assistance (loop not accessible); trailhead: Mirror Lake shuttle bus stop. A paved trail climbs gently along Tenaya Creek to Mirror Lake, a small lake reflecting surrounding cliffs. A loop continues past the lake, crossing the footbridge at Tenaya Creek and returning on the east side of Mirror Lake. The lake is filling in with sediment and is usually dry from late summer to spring, when runoff again fills the basin.

Upper Yosemite Fall: 3.4mi/5.4km one way; 6-8 hrs. roundtrip; strenuous; trailhead: NW corner of Sunnyside Campground parking lot (across street from Yosemite Lodge shuttle bus stop). This trail leads to the top of one of the world's highest waterfalls, 2,425 ft. above the Valley floor. One mile up the trail is Columbia Rock and a beautiful, panoramic view of Yosemite Valley. Hikers should carry water in summer.

Vernal-Nevada Falls Trail: 1.5mi/2.4km to top of Vernal Fall; 3.4mi/5.0km to top of Nevada Fall; 2-4 hrs. roundtrip to Vernal Fall; 6-8 hrs. roundtrip to Nevada Fall; moderate (first mile) then strenuous; trailhead: Happy Isles Bridge. The trail ascends 400 ft. in .8 mi. from the Happy Isles Bridge to the Vernal Fall Bridge, where there is an excellent view of Vernal Fall. Beyond the bridge .2 mi. is the junction of the horse trail, which ascends via a series of switchbacks to the top of Nevada Fall. From the bridge to the top of Vernal Fall via the Mist Trail is a strenuous .7 mi. hike up a rock stairway of more than 500 steps. To reach the top of Nevada Fall from the base, zigzag up to the junction at the top and walk .2 mi. SW to the top of the fall. A roundtrip can be made by crossing the bridge over the Merced River above Nevada Fall and following the horse trail back to Happy Isles.

Half Dome Trail: 16.8mi/26.9km roundtrip; 10-12 hours; strenuous; trailhead: Happy Isles Bridge. After taking the Mist Trail or horse trail to top of Nevada Fall (see above), the trail follows the Merced River toward Little Yosemite and Half Dome (4.5mi/7.5km and 2850ft/869m from the top of Nevada Fall). The last 900ft/274m to the top of Half Dome is a very steep climb up the east side of the granite dome. A cable trailway consisting of two steel ropes about 3 ft. apart, suspended at arm's height from pipes set in the rock, rises 400ft/122m vertically. The top of Half Dome is a fairly level, large, open surface. **Do not start this climb if the cables are down or if there is any chance of rain or lightning.** The cables are down from approximately early October to mid-May.

Four Mile Trail: (Closed in winter) 4.6mi/7.4km one way; 3-4 hours from Yosemite Valley to Glacier Point; strenuous; trailhead: In Yosemite Valley, 1.25mi/2.0km from Yosemite Village on Southside Dr. at Post V 18 (4-Mile Trail parking area); at Glacier Point, from the E end of parking lot. The trail ascends 3200ft/975m, affording outstanding views of Yosemite Valley. Carry water in summer. The hike can be extended by connecting with the Panorama Trail (see description below) to the Valley for total trip of 13mi/20.8km.

From Glacier Point

Pohono Trail: (Closed in winter) 13mi/20.9km one way; 6-8 hrs; moderate; trailhead: Glacier Point (E end of parking lot) or Wawona Tunnel (from small parking area on S side of road). This trail can be taken from either trailhead, or in the other direction (although that direction is primarily uphill), or from the Taft Point/Sentinel Dome trailhead at the turnout on Glacier Point Road (0.1mi N of post G8). The trail follows the south rim of Yosemite Valley, dropping 1800ft/549m. At Taft, Crocker and Dewey points, the trail comes out to the edge of Yosemite Valley, offering outstanding views. This trail is known for its abundant and varied wildflowers in spring and early summer. Carry water.

Panorama Trail: (Closed in winter) 8.5mi/13.7km one way; 4-6 hours (one way to Valley floor); moderate to strenuous with some steep downhill; trailhead: Glacier point (E end of parking lot) or Happy Isles Bridge. From Glacier Point the trail descends 3200ft/975m with some short uphill sections. (The first section of forest, from near the trailhead to Illilouette Falls, was severely damaged by a forest fire in 1986.) The trail crosses Illilouette Fall 1.5mi/2.4km from Glacier Point and continues along the Panorama Cliffs. This 2mi/3.2km portion of the trail offers many scenic views. At the top of Nevada Fall, the trail joins the Vernal-Nevada Falls Trail and continues down to Happy Isles. Carry water.

AUTHOR'S COMMENT: For hiking from Glacier Point to the Valley floor, you might consider taking the bus to Glacier Point for a fee.

From Tuolumne Meadows

Lembert Dome: 1.4mi/2.2km one way; allow 2.5-3 hrs.; strenuous; trailhead: Lembert Dome (Dog Lake) parking area adjacent to CA 120. This is one of the more popular day hikes out of Tuolumne Meadows. It is a short but steep hike (850' ascent) which affords the best view available of the meadows.

Elizabeth Lake: 2.4mi/3.8km one way; allow 2.5-3 hrs.; moderate; trailhead: Tuolumne Meadows Campground. This trail ascends 800 ft. through a lodgepole pine forest before leveling off in a beautiful mountain meadow which cradles this mountain jewel.

Lower Cathedral Lake: 3.8mi/6.1km one way; allow 4-5 hrs; moderate; trailhead: Budd Creek, approximately .75 mi. W of Visitor Center off CA 120. This trail is part of the John Muir Trail westbound. After approximately 3 miles, there is a .75 mi. spur leading to Lower Cathedral's east shore. Continuing 1 mi. on the John Muir Trail brings you to Upper Cathedral Lake.

Backpacking—HIGH SIERRA CAMPS

High Sierra Loop Trail: 50.0mi/80.0km; trailhead: Tuolumne Meadows. The trail passes summer camps (Tuolumne Meadows, Glen Aulin, May Lake, Sunrise, Merced Lake, Vogelsang), which are an average of 1-day's hike apart. In addition, there is White Wolf, located on old Tioga Rd. 1 mile from junction with new Tioga Rd. Camps provide tents, bunk beds, bedding, breakfast and dinner, and dining tent. Reservations are required: High Sierra Camps, Yosemite Park and Curry Co., Yosemite, CA 95389; 209/372-4611.

Park Service permits are not necessary if you are confirmed for the High Sierra Camps.

BRIEF HISTORY

Native Americans lived in the Yosemite Valley area perhaps as many as 4,000 years ago. By the 1850's, when they first made contact with non-Indian people, native residents were mainly the Ahwahneechee of southern Miwok ancestry. Their first recorded contact with non-Indians was with the Mariposa Battalion, which was organized as a punitive expedition against the Indians and entered the Valley on March 25, 1851.

The word soon spread of this wondrous place which became known as "the incomparable valley" throughout the world. Wawona, Miwok for "big tree", was

---

YOSEMITE   **156**

the site of a hostel built in 1857, known for its builder as "Clark's Station." The original Wawona Road was opened in 1875 and the Wawona Hotel was built at this time. The Hotel is still in operation today, which gives thought to the saying, "They don't build 'em like they used to".

Conservationists, at the time headed by Frederick Law Olmsted and I.W. Raymond, were instrumental in having Yosemite Valley and the Mariposa Grove of Giant Sequoias granted to California as a public trust on June 30, 1864. Further efforts led by John Muir resulted in the creation of Yosemite National Park in 1890. The State then ceded its trust to the Federal Government in 1906, thus adding those segments of land to the existing national park area.

In 1914 civilian rangers took over from the military and the National Park Service was established in 1916. Early summer camps were established at this time and were consolidated in the twenties and thirties.

Development of the park continued to accommodate the steadily increasing visitation which today numbers nearly three million. The park's General Management Plan, approved and implemented in 1980, seeks to trim excessive development and upgrade facilities that will remain.

AUTHOR'S COMMENTS

Yosemite is special. "The incomparable valley", as it has been called, is just that. It is a park for all seasons. Spring with melting snows produces thundering spectacular waterfalls. Summer follows with wildflowers replacing the retreating snowpack. Fall brings a wondrous spectrum of color from light yellow to scarlet. Winter brings a mantle of snow sparkling like millions of shimmering diamonds as it glistens from branches of trees and rocks. Ansel Adams, one of the world's foremost photographers, spent much of his lifetime here—and it's no wonder. After all, he had one of the world's most beautiful subjects.

Zion

LOCATION:	Southwestern Utah
ACCESS:	From the west, I-15 to Utah 9 (10 mi. north of St. George) or Utah 17 south of Cedar City; also Kolob Canyons Road off I-15 at Exit 40; from the east, Utah 9 at Mt. Carmel Junction on U.S. 89
SEASON:	All year; Kolob Terrace Road closed in winter, but Zion-Mt. Carmel, Zion Canyon Scenic and Kolob Canyons Roads are kept open.
HOURS:	24 hours/day
ENTRANCE FEES:	$5/vehicle/week; $2/person all others/week; $15 annual; $25 Golden Eagle
FOOD & LODGING:	ZION LODGE: open April to November; cabins; restaurant; snack bar; auditorium; gift shop; reservations: TW Services, Inc., 451 N. Main St., Cedar City, UT 84720; 801/586-7686
GAS:	Springdale,Hurricane,La Verkin,Kanab, St. George, Cedar City
NEAREST PROPANE:	Springdale
CAMPGROUNDS:	2 developed campgrounds; 1 primitive; no hook-ups; group camping; dump stations
ADJACENT FACILITIES:	See below
VISITOR CENTERS:	Zion Canyon Visitor Center near South Entrance to Park; Kolob Canyons Visitor Center at Kolob Canyons Exit 40 from I-15
MUSEUM:	In Zion Canyon Visitor Center (also bookstore)
PICNICKING:	Grotto Picnic Area; Kolob Canyons
GIFT SHOP:	In Zion Lodge
TOURS:	Naturalist-guided walks and hikes (some off-trail hikes); guided horseback trips; tram tours
ACTIVITIES:	Hiking; mountain climbing (optional registration); interpretive programs; Zion Nature Center (Junior Ranger Program for children 6 through 12); fishing (license required)
CLIMATE:	Hot summers; mild winters
ELEVATION:	3,650 to 8,740 ft.
SIZE:	230 sq. miles
ANNUAL VISITATION:	Approximately two million
PETS:	Must be on leash; not permitted on trails or in backcountry
FACILITIES FOR DISABLED:	Most public facilities; campsites; restrooms
INFORMATION:	*Supt. Zion National Park* *Springdale, UT 84767-1099* 801/772-3256 *Park emergency:* 801/772-3322 *or* 772-3311

In Springdale (just outside South Entrance to Park): Complete commercial facilities; write Chamber of Commerce, P.O. Box 111, Springdale, UT 84767

East Zion RV Park: At Mt. Carmel Junction Hwy. 89 & 9; open 3/15-11/30; full hook-ups; propane; dump station; reserv. P.O. Box 17, Mt. Carmel Junction, UT 84775

Zion Canyon C.G.: In Springdale; open all year; full hook-ups; showers; flush toilets; sanitary dump station; store; cafe; laundry; ice; reserv. Box 99, Springdale, UT 84767; 801/772-3237

Robert's Roost TRL Pk: In Hurricane; open all year; full hook-ups; showers; flush toilets; reserv. Box 476, Hurricane, UT 84737; 801/635-4476

KOA *Black Rock* RV Park: At junction of Utah 17 and Hwy. 9; open all year; full hook-ups; showers; flush toilets; propane; dump station; store; laundry; ice; reserv. P.O. Box 160, La Verkin, UT 84745; 801/635-4272

Gateway Trailer & RV Park: At junction of Hwy. 9 & 17; open all year; full hook-ups; showers; flush toilets; propane; store; cafe; laundry; ice; reserv. Box 129, La Verkin, UT 84743; 801/635-4533

CAMPGROUNDS

- All campsites have tables and firegrates.
- Camping is on a first-come basis with a 14-day limit of stay.
- Dead and down firewood may be gathered.

South Campground (elev. 4000') is located one mile beyond the South Entrance to the Park in a grassy, shaded area next to the Virgin River. It has 140 sites and is open all year when Watchman Campground is closed for the winter. The campground fee is $5. Facilities include water and flush toilets, telephones, an amphitheater with evening programs, and a dump station. Swimming and tubing are available in the adjacent Virgin River. The campground is useable for handicapped. Showers, stores, tube rentals, etc. are available in Springdale, just outside the Park entrance.

Watchman Campground (elev. 4000') is located one mile south of South Campground in a spacious, shady area next to the Virgin River with 228 sites. It is open all year when South Campground is closed for the winter. Group camping is available with prior reservations for organized groups. The campground fee is $5. Facilities include water and flush toilets, telephones, an amphitheater with evening programs, and a dump station. Swimming and tubing are available in the River. The campground is useable for handicapped.

Lava Point Primitive Campground (elev. 7850') is located at Lava Point. It consists of 6 sites and is usually open May to October, depending on the weather. Facilities include pit toilets. There is *no water* at the campground.

HIKING

Self-Guiding Trails (All distances are one way)

Weeping Rock: .25mi/.4km; 30 minutes round trip; easy; 98' ascent; trailhead: Weeping Rock parking area. This is a great hike for families with small children or the elderly. It has a natural shower at the end with small drops that you can dodge or not. Children will enjoy the natural wading pool at the bottom of the trail; but most of all they will enjoy learning all about the trees and plants along the way. There are beautiful hanging gardens of wildflowers and other flora looking like bonsai trees growing out of the rock.

Canyon Overlook: 0.5mi/0.8km; one hour round trip; easy; 163' ascent; trailhead: across the highway from the parking lot at the east end of the Zion-Mt. Carmel Tunnel. This self-guiding trail has leaflets available at trailhead and offers views of Zion Canyon, West Temple and Pine Creek Canyon.

Gateway to the Narrows: 1.0mi/1.6km; 1½ to 2 hours round trip; easy; 57' ascent; trailhead: Temple of Sinawava at the end of Zion Canyon Scenic Drive. This beautiful, paved trail follows the Virgin River until it ends at The Narrows. This hike is a must! During the spring and summer months, the canyon walls are covered with such wildflowers as columbine, cardinal flower and shooting stars with a backdrop of maidenhair fern. Naturalist-guided hikes are available from April through October. The trail is suitable for wheelchairs or strollers, and wading is popular. There are flush toilets and water at the trailhead.

*   *   *   *   *

Emerald Pools: to LOWER POOL .6mi/1.0km; to MIDDLE POOL 1.0mi/1.6km; to UPPER POOL 1.3mi/2.1km; 2½ hours; easy; 69' ascent to Lower Pool; trailheads: Zion Lodge or Grotto Picnic Area. After crossing the picturesque bridge over the Virgin River across from Zion Lodge, you may trail to the left to Middle Pool or the right to Lower Pool. In my opinion, the best way is to hike to Middle Pool, then to Upper Pool, return to Lower Pool, and complete loop by

---

returning to Grotto Picnic Area. Naturalist-guided tours are available from April through October. Zion Lodge to Lower Pool is suitable for wheelchairs and strollers. There's a free waterfall shower at Lower Pool.

Hidden Canyon: 1.5mi/2.4km; 3 hours; strenuous; 850' ascent; trailhead: Weeping Rock parking area. The trail ends at the canyon entrance, but the hike may be continued into the canyon. The entrance to the canyon is almost hidden from view from the Zion Canyon floor, thus the name "Hidden Canyon".

Sand Bench: 1.7mi/2.7km; 3 hours; moderate; 500' ascent; trailhead: Court of Patriarchs. The trail follows Birch Creek, then turns left crossing the creek and continues climbing to the bench above. The hike includes views of the Watchman, Three Patriarchs and Pine Creek Canyon. It is not recommended in summer months due to heavy horse use.

Watchman: 1.2mi/1.9km; 2 hours; moderate; 368' ascent; trailhead: South Campground amphitheater or bridge. This trail is best hiked fall through spring. It ends above Watchman Campground.

Angels Landing: 2.5mi/4.0km; 4 hours round trip; strenuous; 1488' ascent; trailhead: Grotto Picnic Area parking lot. It ends at Angels Landing.

West Rim: 6.0mi/9.6km to West Rim Overlook; 1 day round trip. 13.3mi/21.3km to Lava Point; 2 days round trip; strenuous; 3593' ascent; trailhead: Grotto Picnic Area. This is one of Zion's best backpacking trails, with a primitive campground at Lava Point, the trail's end. An alternative hike is to drive to Lava Point and hike down to canyon floor for pick up. The trail has a descent of 3600 ft.

East Rim: 4.0mi/6.4km; 6 hours; strenuous; 2148' ascent; trailhead: Weeping Rock parking area. This trail ascends up Echo Canyon, ending at Observation Point.

Taylor Creek: 2.7mi/4.4km to Double Arch Alcove; 4 hours; moderate; trailhead: 2 miles from Kolob Canyon Entrance.

BRIEF HISTORY

The first-known inhabitants of the area were the Anasazi Indians. They abandoned the area around A.D. 1200. The Paiutes used the area for hunting, but there were no further permanent residents until the middle 1800's.

During Major Powell's second voyage down the Colorado River in 1871, the region was explored and mapped. His protegé, Major C. E. Dutton, along with Captain George Wheeler, completed mapping the area now in the Park. It was declared a national monument on July 31, 1909 by President William Howard Taft and established as a national park on November 19, 1919.

In 1923 a wagon road was graded as far as Weeping Rock. Access from the east at this time was over Rockville Mountain. The Zion-Mt. Carmel Highway, which is highlighted by the Pine Creek Tunnel, was dedicated July 4, 1930.

AUTHOR'S COMMENTS

Zion National Park has been described in reverence as "a temple of God". Another description is that it "looks like Yosemite in color". Both are apt.

Although Zion looks like Yosemite, its formation is quite different. The

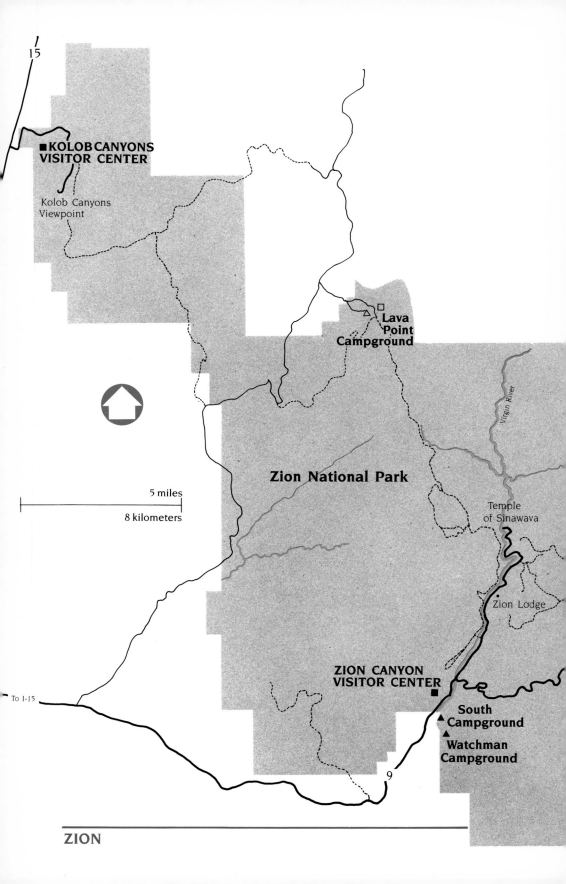

15

■ **KOLOB CANYONS
VISITOR CENTER**

Kolob Canyons
Viewpoint

△ □ **Lava
Point
Campground**

Virgin River

Zion National Park

5 miles

8 kilometers

Temple
of Sinawava

Zion Lodge

To I-15

**ZION CANYON
VISITOR CENTER**
■

▲ **South
Campground**

▲ **Watchman
Campground**

9

ZION

main carving force at Yosemite was glaciers, whereas at Zion it was and is the Virgin River cutting through the soft Navajo sandstone.

The author suggests that to get the kinks out of your neck from looking up at Zion, you next visit the North Rim of Grand Canyon National Park and start looking down.

East
Entrance

9

About the Author

George Perkins was born in Chicago, Illinois and graduated from New Trier High School in Winnetka, Illinois. He also graduated from the University of Colorado with a degree in business administration. He enlisted in the Korean War and served with Hawaii's famous 5th regimental combat team. He attended officer candidate school at Fort Riley, Kansas and was commissioned a 2nd Lieutenant in 1952. He has three daughters: Heidi, Lynn, and Jody. He currently owns and operates "The Ski Renter," a chain of ski rental shops in the Western United States. He maintains a home in Mineral where he "summers." For comments or information, his address is Box 129, Mineral, California 96063.

Photos, text, research and editorial . . . . George Perkins, Mineral, CA
Design, production . . . . Carole Thickstun, Tubac, AZ
Typesetting . . . . Typecraft, Tucson, AZ
Printing . . . . Lorraine Press, Salt Lake City, UT
Color separations . . . . TruColour, Phoenix, AZ

Mariposa Lily

Mountain Mule Ears

False Hellebore

Brodiaea

California Stickseed

Water Buttercup